D1552514

THE 5 KEYS
TO THE GREAT LIFE

DR. TOMI BRYAN
DR. JERRY WHITE
With *foreword* by Denise Linn

R2 MEDIA GROUP PUBLICATIONS

R2 MEDIA GROUP PUBLICATIONS
A division of R2 Media Group
315 W. Center Street Suite 302
Pocatello, ID 83204
www.r2mg.com

Designed By R2 Media Group
Printed in the United States of America.

ISBN 13: 978-0-9824587-0-9
ISBN 10: 0-9824587-0-3

Excerpts of *"The Divine Matrix: Bridging Time, Space, Miracles,
and Belief"* copyright 2007 by Gregg Braden, reprinted by
permission of Hay House, Inc. Carlsbad, CA.

Original artwork for cover by John Schweitzer

For

Jim, Shep and Warren.

Always the light in my darkness.

—*Tomi*

For

Janice, Nate and Em.

Their sacrifice for me is their greatest gift.

—*Jerry*

Acknowledgements

A book is clearly a community project and this one was no different. In general, I am grateful to be the one, along with Jerry, to be the steward of the great life. I enjoyed every second of hanging out with you, Jerry, as we wrote this book. I am grateful to my husband, Jim, and children, Shep and Warren, for the sacrifices they made and the material they provided just by being themselves. The three of you have always encouraged me to be all that I am. Thanks to mom and Mike. No matter how much of a crazymaker I was, you loved me anyway. Your unconditional love has been a magnificent gift. Finally, every Batman (or woman) needs a Robin to make it all happen. Thanks for being my Robin, Judy!

—*Tomi*

This book has been an accumulation of effort and ideas from people who were sharing of their time, their thoughts, and their wisdom. Many being the authors and ancestors that went before us. I am fortunate enough to share my great life with my wife Janice and children Amanda, Austin, Nathan, and Emily, and great colleagues like Al, Jane, Shane, and Ryan. Everyone's support in this effort has kept me moving forward. I am especially honored that I was able to spend time with my mother, Janie, and brother, Mike, on my trips to NC as my sister, Tomi, and I explored the universe and took mental journeys through time from the comfort of the "thought table."

—Jerry

Table of Contents

A Note From Tomi

My father's death on February 6, 1998, took me to one of the lowest points in my life. I was crushed that I didn't know how to say goodbye to him, to honor his life, and to let him go. I loved him deeply throughout my life, but even more ferociously during the last awful six months when cancer ravaged his strength, his body, and his mind. To feel such despair over my dad's dying coupled with a longing to say goodbye without the tools to do so, spun my life out of control. He was a powerful anchor in my life and now he was gone.

Dad's death was the catalyst for my quest to understand life and my role in it. "Is this all there is?" I wondered shortly after his death. Was I brought here for a greater purpose and had I missed the chance to fulfill my destiny? In the 10 years following my father's death, I went in search of my purpose. As we like to say in the leadership world, I began to stalk my longing. I needed to make my life better, but I had no idea how to do that. I read countless books, attended many training sessions, and went to workshops all over the country, searching for a theory capable of describing the world and my place in it in one, coherent structure. Everything I read offered a gem or two, but never satisfied my need for, nor my belief that there was, an operating system for life.

Fast forward to January 2008 when my brother, Mike, and my mother, Janie, became deathly ill at the same time. Janie and Mike stayed in my living room for six months while their bodies decided which path they wanted to take. Since we didn't know what Janie and Mike's fates were, our family encircled them. My brother, Jerry, and my sister, Janie, spent a lot of time at my house during Operation Mike and Janie. I felt so fortunate to have long discussions with Jerry and Janie about my dad, Tom, and about life in general. It was during one of these conversations with Jerry that we developed the idea for this book. Jerry and I began to sit at the thought table (the conference room table at my office in Greensboro, North Carolina). The thought table is where amazing conversations take place and magical things happen. Eventually, those conversations around that table shaped and formed The Great Life System presented here.

We invited my business partner, Judy Johnson, to sit at the thought table with us. There were three of us at the table but four chairs. One day I asked myself who was sitting in that fourth chair at the thought table. I began to imagine great authors and thinkers sitting in that fourth chair, offering us their wisdom and guidance and cheering us on. From that moment forward I imagined Thomas Jefferson, Benjamin Franklin, Henry David Thoreau, the Sufi poet Hafiz, Lao-tzu, Einstein, Shakespeare, Mark Twain, and other greats sitting in that chair (not all at the same time as that would have been a little crowded). Often I asked for their advice and pondered what they might do in my situation. The feeling of their presence offered me peace, tranquility, and knowing that what I was working on was significant.

It is my desire that the keys shared here help you find what is significant and meaningful. May your great life be right around the corner!

A Note From Jerry

The shortest path between two points is a straight line. However, I have never traveled that straight line. Two songs come to mind when I try to describe my journey to my Great Life, "The Long and Winding Road" by the Beatles and "Bless the Broken Road" by Rascal Flatts. My journey has taken many twists and turns to get where I am now—and I wouldn't trade that for anything. I have been fortunate to work in many fields (psychology, technology, education, government, management, and the corn field). These career choices have taken me to many locations, and they all provided opportunities for me to grow and learn. I have met many influential people along my journey and have learned valuable life lessons from them—some I took to heart which allowed me to change my life. Obviously, the most important was my father. He laid the foundation for much of the work Tomi and I have accomplished in this book. His dedication, sharing, and compassion for helping people provided a compass for me to find my way. He taught me to ask questions, explore, and research to find answers and not be afraid to forge ahead.

It was the intersection of catastrophic events in my and others' lives that brought everything together in January of 2008. My mother was having medical problems, my brother almost died twice, and I traveled to North Carolina frequently to be with family. It was during one of these visits that my sister and I sat in my brother's hospital room in the ICU and discussed the meaning and purpose of life. We also questioned why everyone could not have a great life. It was in those moments that Tomi, with her organizational management and systems thinking background, and I, with my psychology and education background, began to merge our ideas and research into *The 5 Keys to the Great Life* and The Great Life System. The outgrowth of those meetings has changed my life. My mother and my brother are still with us and Tomi and I are sharing the keys to the Great Life with you. It is a great life!

Foreword *By Denise Linn*

We live in a transformative time. Everything is changing so fast. At this point the things that freshmen are learning in technical colleges are outdated by the time they are juniors. The speed of change in our culture is breathtaking.

I was very close with my husband's grandmother until she died at a wonderful old age. Hattie was an amazing source of information. She talked about what it was like growing up before the invention of the automobile when the only way to get around was a horse. Even my mother, who was born a couple of years after the first mass-assembly automobile, remembers that when she was a child the only way she and her family got around was with horse and buggy. Hattie also talked about the excitement surrounding the invention of the first airplanes and how they revolutionized life by making the world a seemingly smaller place.

I personally can remember the invention of the television. As a kid I thought it was a magical box. I believed there were little people inside the box and I circled around and around the television trying to find a way to get them to come out and play with me. Now televisions, computers, and cell phones are second nature to everyone. I've watched a two-and-a-half year old child turn on a computer and begin to navigate to his favorite sites. I've seen people hiking in the woods talking on cell phones to someone halfway around the world. From a historical perspective, all of this has happened so quickly.

When I was in Australia a number of years ago, I met an aboriginal woman whom—until she was ten years old—lived exactly the same as her ancestors 2,000 years ago. (The aboriginal tools had not advanced in all those years.) Imagine what it would be like to go from living in an ancient tribal way as a child to flying on airplanes and talking on cell phones and watching *YouTube*… all within one lifetime.

Within just over a century, the fabric of our lives has changed dramatically. And, the advances in technology are growing exponentially. The genetic DNA programming from thousands of years of ancestry no longer serves the needs of our rapidly changing modern times. In many ways, it's as if we are small boats, with our anchors cut, out on a stormy sea. The reassurances of what worked in the past to overcome life's challenges, no longer serve us today.

It is especially during these times that we need anchors to allow us to remain stable and secure as the whirlwinds of change whip at our core. The remarkable thing about the book that Tomi and her brother, Jerry, have crafted is that through weathering their own personal storms, they have discovered strategies and modalities to assist us to be balanced in these uncertain times, and to step forward to become leaders and light houses for others amidst the storm. They understand the potency of the human spirit and how each of us can harness that power for our own health and well-being and also how we can support others to find their own light.

As you do the exercises in this book, you will learn how to be the compassionate observer without becoming embroiled in the drama of life. You will also discover how to truly know what your soul yearns for and how to find the path amidst the white water of confusion.

For some, these times will be destructive to their human spirit; yet, for others these times of chaos will bring new growth and vitality, the way a storm at sea churns up nutrients from the ocean floor for the creatures above.

To find your sparkle and joy in these times, I suggest whole heartedly embracing the exercises and suggestions in this well crafted book so that the years ahead are the best years of your life.

Denise Linn • Paso Robles, California

Be sure to visit Hay House author, Denise Linn, at www.deniselinn.com. Her book titles include the following: *Four Acts of Personal Power: How to Heal Your Past and Create a Positive Future, The Soul Loves the Truth: Lessons Learned on the Path to Joy, If I Can Forgive, So Can You: My Autobiography of How I Overcame My Past And Healed My Life, Soul Coaching, Secrets and Mysteries, The Glory and Pleasure of being a Woman, Feng Shui for the Soul, Space Clearing A-Z, Sacred Space, Secret Language of Signs, Past Lives, Present Dreams, Hidden Power of Dreams, Quest, Altars: Bringing Sacred Shrines into your Everyday Life, Space Clearing*

Denise Linn can also be heard on Hay House Radio at http://www.hayhouseradio.com

Preface: Suggestions on How to Read this Book

Before embarking on the path to your great life, we (Jerry and Tomi) feel it necessary to share with you the design of this book. Without a doubt, we see Chapter 6, *How to Coach the Team*, as the bellwether of the book. Chapter 6, along with Chapter 5, are the *hows* of the great life. At the most basic level, life is about "know-how." We get the *know* through many methods, including watching the way machines function, reading books, listening to compact discs, watching others, or having theory taught to us. The *how* is derived from taking action on the know. We act on the know to get the how. This methodology is the traditional way of learning. Throughout school, we typically learned the history and theory of a topic, and then we learned how to apply it. As part-time academicians and full-time mad scientists, Jerry and Tomi have designed this book in that traditional way. First, we offer the theory of the great life (the know) and then we move to methods of application (the how). If you are the type of person who is interested only in the how, then we suggest you start reading at Chapter 5, *How to Use the Looking Glass*, as Chapter 5 and Chapter 6 offer many of the hows. Having said that, we advise against skipping directly to Chapter 5 or Chapter 6, though, as Chapters 1, 2, 3, and 4 are necessary building blocks for the great life and are integral parts of living the great life. Regardless of how you choose to approach reading this book, we know your great life is waiting for you on the next page, whichever one that is!

THE 5 KEYS
TO THE GREAT LIFE

DR. TOMI BRYAN
DR. JERRY WHITE
With *foreword* by Denise Linn

R2 MEDIA GROUP PUBLICATIONS

CHAPTER 1

Introduction

Key [kee]

something that affords a means of access: the key to happiness; something that secures or controls entrance to a place: Gibraltar is the key to the Mediterranean; something that affords a means of clarifying a problem; the system, method, pattern, etc., used to decode or decipher a cryptogram, as a code book, machine setting, or key word. (http://dictionary.reference.com/browse/key)

> *If you want real success, it's very likely that some of your old patterns won't work for you any longer.*
>
> *—Sandra Anne Taylor*

It is a great day to start your great life. The five keys highlighted in this book will allow you to do just that: start your great life. The challenge is doing so in the permanent whitewater in which we currently find ourselves and our businesses. Permanent whitewater consists of "social, economic and political environments that are fraught with the risk of rapid change. Such environments require a different mode of organization, information processing, and leadership skills from the traditional forms of management and control" (Comfort, Sungo, Johnson, & Dunn, 2001, p. 144). The complexity of day-to-day life is overwhelming and overpowering us:

> Perhaps for the first time in history, humankind has the capacity to create far more information than anyone can absorb, to foster far greater interdependency than anyone can manage, and to accelerate change far faster than anyone's ability to keep pace. Certainly the scale of complexity is without precedent. All around us are examples of "systemic breakdowns"—problems such as global warming, ozone depletion, the international drug trade, and the U.S. trade and budget deficits—problems that have no simple local cause. (Senge, 1994, p. 69)

Remarkably, it is quite likely that no century before the last one endured such rapid, ongoing, and radical change. Society is in a period of transition like no other. Peter Drucker (1998) summarized this time of transition best:

> Every few hundred years throughout Western history, a sharp transformation has occurred. In a matter of decades, society altogether rearranges itself—its worldview, its basic values, its social and political structures, its arts, its key institutions. Fifty years later a new world exists. And the people born into that world cannot even imagine the world in which their grandparents lived and into which their own parents were born.
>
> Our age is such a period of transformation. (p. 75)

In his book *The Third Wave*, Alvin Toffler (1980) wrote, "A powerful tide is surging across much of the world today, creating a new, often bizarre, environment in which to work, play, marry, raise children, or retire" (p. 18). He referred to this powerful tide as "the death of industrialism and the rise of a new civilization" (Toffler, p. 18); a third wave of change. The other two waves of change in history have been the development of agriculture and the Industrial Revolution. Toffler (1980) described the new civilization that would emerge from this third wave of change:

> So profoundly revolutionary is this new civilization that it challenges all our old assumptions. Old ways of thinking, old formulas, dogmas, and ideologies, no matter how cherished or how useful in the past, no longer fit the facts. The world that is fast emerging from the clash of new values and technologies, new geopolitical relationships, new life-styles and modes of communication, demands wholly new ideas and analogies, classifications and concepts. We cannot cram the embryonic world of tomorrow into yesterday's conventional cubbyholes. (p. 18)

Jerry and Tomi believe the impact and effects of this transformational period have finally filtered down to the individual level. Just like the chaos in organizations, we now see constant systemic breakdowns in our personal lives. Society continues to grapple with a high divorce rate; it is not uncommon to meet people who are on their third or fourth marriage. Single parent families and mixed families (step- and half-siblings) have become the norm. Some of us haven't spoken to certain family members in months or years, because they offended us at the last family gathering or they spoke a truth we didn't want to hear. Moreover, we have good friends that no longer speak to us and we don't know why. We have no faith in our leaders, our religions or our bosses. We have lost jobs that we shouldn't have, and we are angry. Our bank accounts and retirement plans are a debris field. We experience road rage with minimal provocation. Our lives are breaking down and many of us are unhappy at our core. Fun is rarely even an afterthought. Yes, that sounds like permanent whitewater to us. How are we to cope with such comprehensive change and turmoil? How are we to cope with this accelerated change?

In case the above examples of permanent whitewater don't convince you a new approach to life is necessary, maybe these documented facts from Tommy Newberry's 2007 book, *Success is not an Accident*, will:

1.   Currently, 49 percent of marriages end in divorce.

2.   More than 80 percent of the people working today would rather be in another line of work.

3.   More than 50 percent of Americans are overweight.

4.   One out of three Americans will get cancer, and two out of five will suffer from heart disease.

5.   More than 60 percent of Americans who live in the richest, most abundant civilization in history will retire with little or no savings and will become dependent on so-called entitlements for survival. (p. xiv)

So many of us see our lives as headed in the wrong direction but we don't know what to do about it. As Fritz (1991) described it:

> Let's face it, most of us have the suspicion there is much more to life than what we have been led to expect. Our lives are filled with secret possibilities—possibilities that there are dimensions to ourselves, depths of our being, and heights to our aspirations that are lurking just below the surface. Despite years of attempts by relatives, friends, acquaintances and society to bring us to our senses, the desire and impulse to reach for that which is highest in us is still there. After all the appeals to reason, we still have the very human urge to do something that matters to us. Despite all the times that society has endeavored to kill that instinct in us, it just won't die. (p. 3)

Many of us have no mechanism for discovering those aspirations lurking just below the surface. We have no idea how to identify what we want out of life, much less what we want to truly create for ourselves. World renowned medical intuitive and author Carolyn Myss (2007) has a compact disc set called *Your Power to Create* in which she talks about creating what we want in life. Myss talks about the fact that most of us have no clue about what we want. Sure we all want world peace and to find a cure for cancer, but what is it that you really want? At the personal level, what do you want? Myss says that most of us can't answer that question. Tomi conducted her own informal survey and discovered that most of the people she met during her travels over a 30 day period couldn't answer the question either.

Tomi has a very personal example of not being able to find what lurks below the surface. The death of Tomi's dad in 1998 at the young age of 65 meant her best friend of 33 years was gone. She felt adrift, sad, lonely, and lost. The experience made her ask quietly on the inside, "Is this all there is to life?" But her head and heart were louder, screaming at her in unison, "You are supposed to be doing something more, what is it?" It was only after her dad passed away that Tomi learned through conversations with her mother, Janie, that her father often talked about his sense that he was supposed to be doing something but he did not know what it was. Tomi's dad died not knowing what that something was or at least not recognizing the value of his own life. The revelation by Janie that Tomi's dad was searching for something made the search for the vision for her life even more important. How could you get to 65 years old and not know what you were supposed to be doing? Or, how could you get to 65 years old and not have the understanding to know that you had fulfilled your life purpose? Jerry and Tomi don't want you to be at the end of your life still wondering what you are supposed to be doing. In this book, we help you cover that ground.

So many times when we are in the middle of a permanent whitewater moment, we cannot see which direction we are headed, much less that it is the wrong direction. The complexity of the situation clouds our vision, which might include engaging in old patterns of behavior that keep us locked in the same cycle, interference from our own emotions or emotions of others, or even baggage from the past that interjects itself into the moment. For years we have been *winging it* in our personal lives, and that no longer works. With the increased chaos and complexity facing us each day, we can't continue to operate the same way. Existing solutions, patterns, and habits won't help us navigate the permanent whitewater coursing through our lives. We rarely know how to change. We scarcely know how to be honest—with ourselves and with others. We seldom know how to forgive. For these reasons, we need new tools, strategies, and resources to help us impose order on this chaos. We need some means to sort through the complexity. We need to understand how to live with conscious intention.

Regardless of centuries of inquiry into the field of human endeavors, we still wait on an example of how to live our lives. Despite all we face in this new century, no field of human endeavor has yet to offer us a practical system that identifies our own personal universe, what is in it, and how we can live intentionally within that space. Not philosophy. Not psychology. No field of study has yet to offer us even a basic model that provides clarity to where we stand relative to everything else in our world. Not sociology. Not cultural anthropology. Until now.

But why should you care? Because when we live without understanding the structure we function in, we don't make informed choices. We don't use the system to our advantage. Instead, the forces of the system toss curve balls at us. Some of us just stand in front of the automatic pitching machine known as Life while it keeps hurling balls at us as fast as it can. Because we have no strategies for living, we don't even know how to move from in front of the machine. In fact, so many of us wait until life throws us a catastrophic curve ball before we wake up to our destiny and the great life that is waiting for us.

A lot of great people had to have extreme curve balls thrown at them before finding their great lives. Author Jerry White (2008) (not the co-author of this book) calls these life moments *dates with destiny*. Author and leadership expert John Maxwell (2008) calls them *defining moments*. Regardless of what you call them, we all experience such moments.

A land mine blew White's leg off when he was 20. In *I Will Not Be Broken* (2008), he talked about "people who, through no fault of their own, had slammed into some kind of horrible date with destiny" (p. 2). White also talked about how these dates with destiny divide life in two—everything that came before that date, and everything that came after that date. He poignantly described these life-altering events:

> It's not enough to survive these life shattering moments; we must live through them and move forward after them. Everyone, if not now then eventually, has a date—the day something blows up in your face, dividing life into before and after. Things are never quite the same when the dust and debris settle. (p. 14)

Everyone has such dates and "these dates weren't always tragic times, but times that fundamentally changed a person, a family, a community" (p. 16). According to White, "our dates are unforgettable because they change not only the facts of our lives—*I used to have a leg*—but our worldview and self concept—*I come from a broken home*. They force us to redefine our expectations and attitude toward life" (p. 17). Sometimes it takes a date with destiny for us to fulfill our life purpose and to understand what life expects from us. It is the universe's poignant way of causing us to course correct.

Leadership expert John Maxwell (2008) categorized these dates with destiny as ground breakers, heart breakers, cloud breakers, and chart breakers. To him, they are *defining moments*. In *Leadership Gold*, Maxwell wrote the following about defining moments:

> You will never be the same person after a defining moment. Somehow you will be moved. It may be forward, or it may be backward, but make no mistake—you will be moved. Why is that? Because defining moments are not normal, and what's "normal" doesn't work in those times.
>
> I think of defining moments as intersections in our lives. They give us an opportunity to turn, change direction, and seek a new destination. They present options and opportunities. In these moments, we must choose. And the choice we make will define us! What will we do? Our response puts us on a new path, and that new path will define who we will become in the future. After a defining moment, we will never be the same person again. (pp. 22-23)

In *People Are Idiots and I Can Prove It*, Larry Winget (2009) takes a more practical approach to these dates with destiny, writing that habits or destructive patterns become important enough to change only when it is either too late or almost too late. He advises taking action now, commenting that "It's imperative that you determine what is important to you before a tragedy happens. That way you can begin to spend your time, energy and money on the things that matter" (p. 49).

Many of us are caught in the permanent whitewater, acting out of habit with no idea how to change the course of our ride. At least not until the boat tips over, or we lose our paddles, or all of our provisions, or someone falls out of our boat and is gone forever. We are operating in chaos in a universe that appreciates order. And, we stay grounded in our habits until something catastrophic shocks us to the core.

That statement is worth repeating: the universe appreciates order. The human race appreciates order. And, with all the chaos and complexity, we need more order. This means we need some structure. Whether we recognize it or not, all things operate in a system or a structure. For instance, earth is part of a structure called a solar system. You are part of a system called a family. Your children attend a school within a school system.

A great place to see systems in action is sports. To figure out the system, we have to first know which sport. Let's pick American football. From that decision, we know we need a certain type of field: one that is a 100 yards long, marked in 10 yard increments. That field also needs goal posts at both ends. We also need a ball and not just any ball. One that we can pass, catch, kick and punt. We need a certain number of players for offense and a certain number of players for defense. There are specific rules for football that don't apply to other sports. The rules identify what we can do and where the limits are. And, if we exceed the limits, there are penalties. But, you're beginning to get the picture—simply by picking the sport, our minds engage a specific system that we know this sport operates in. We can build expectations around the system. We can produce winners through this system. The good news is life operates in the same manner.

Whether you recognize it or not, everyone—regardless of culture, religion, socioeconomic background or education—operates in the same life system. Jerry and his father, Tom, were the early pioneers of this system. While psychologists in private practice, they began to notice similarities among their clients' life challenges. Couples came for counseling and the tensions between the parties resulted from familiar ground: She didn't like his friends; she spent too much money; he cheated on me; his mother was wreaking havoc on the relationship; or they were of different faiths and how would they raise their children? Individuals came for counseling and their challenges were in the same realms: I don't like myself; I am overweight; I am not loveable; what am I doing with my life; I hate my job; my family doesn't understand me; or why isn't the Creator helping me in my time of need? Jerry and Tom began to categorize these life challenges which led to the realization that these issues originated in one of six dimensions: self, family, faith, fun, finances, or friends. Jerry and Tomi began to refer to these dimensions as the Self and the 5Fs. The root cause was clear: clients didn't like their current reality, for whatever reason; thus, a change in thinking, attitudes, or behaviors was necessary to restore balance to the relationship or to the individual.

As Jerry and Tomi took up where Jerry and Tom left off, they came to understand the six dimensions of Self and the 5Fs, and your relationship to each, represent your personal universe. They are the life system in which you function. Jerry and Tomi named this structure The Great Life System. In *The 5 Keys to the Great Life*, we explain why The Great Life System is the specific system in which you operate and how the choices you make and the laws you live by influence the function of that system. Understanding this system and the 5 keys to its operation gives you the power to control your life and positively expand every aspect of your life. You can use this system to shift your stance on life from one of waiting for those catastrophic events that push you toward your destiny, to one of creating your own destiny—a life stance that is better able to manage such events.

The Great Life System offers a comprehensive view of both yourself and the universe that surrounds you. Understanding this system provides you with a new level of inner power. By knowing the system, you have the power to leverage it to impose more order, more richness, and more fullness to any situation in your life. In short, this system helps you see through the permanent whitewater to enhance the clarity of your choices and decisions. It helps you go about the work of building your great life.

The framework of The Great Life System is the six dimensions of Self and the 5Fs. The six dimensions collaborate to create your personal universe. To maximize your potential in the six dimensions, there are five keys that must be applied:

Key 1: *Know the System*

Key 2: *Know the Language*

Key 3: *Know the Mental Models*

Key 4: *How to Use the Looking Glass*

Key 5: *How to Coach the Team*

Chapter 2 discusses the key that is the basic system for The Great Life System. Chapter 3 and Chapter 4 refer to the keys that explain structural operation of the system and examine the external and internal influences on the system itself. Chapters 5 and 6 refer to the keys that are the personal operation of the system, addressing how the Self should guide that dimension (internal) and how it should guide the other 5 dimensions (external). Chapter 7 synthesizes the system and its uses to help you more fully take action toward your great life. There are tools, strategies and resources in several of the Chapters. If you are committed to a great life, then skimming the tools, strategies and resources won't do. You must practice them as the intent is to encourage you to engage in truthful and deep self-reflection and self-examination to raise your awareness of what your life looks like in this moment. Awareness of where you are is the starting point for where you want to go. By understanding and using the five keys of The Great Life System, its six dimensions and the structural conflicts that may show up, you can discover the great life. Our methods and processes for making this discovery are so easy and practical you will wonder why you didn't find the great life sooner.

The Great Life System is the culmination of Jerry's work in the field of psychology and Tomi's work in the field of systems thinking. Most people have heard of Freud or Jung and many of us consider ourselves amateur psychologists, but few of us have been exposed to systems thinking. Systems thinking is the science of understanding how systems operate. While variations on systems thinking have been around for some time, it was Peter Senge (1994), in his seminal book *The Fifth Discipline,* who popularized the application of systems thinking in the field of management as a methodology for creating and sustaining a unique kind of company called the learning organization. We dig deeper into systems thinking in the next chapter when we introduce The Great Life System.

While the structure of the great life is premised upon systems thinking, the keys of *The 5 Keys to the Great Life* are also rooted in psychological theory with some physics thrown in for good measure. Jerry and Tomi take the time to simplify these theories into practical applications. This book is not intended to replace counseling or a prescribed program by your doctor. Though, it will offer you awareness and understanding of the dynamic forces at work in your life that may be preventing you from living the great life.

There are many personal development books available for improving any facet of your life. But *The 5 Keys to the Great Life* is not your regular self-improvement book. There are few, if any, such books that attempt to tackle more than one life issue at a time. A book on marriage may improve your relationship with your spouse but doesn't necessarily improve your finances. The same with a self-help book on finances—it may improve your bank account but it doesn't necessarily improve your relationship with your spouse. The system detailed in this book is unique. The Great Life System represents the system that is your entire personal universe. The system can be used to address any issue that you may be facing in your life. Finally, you have a book that offers you tools, strategies, and resources for sorting through the complexity. Finally, you have a practical system that identifies your personal universe and what is in it. Finally, you have a system that provides real-time clarity on where you stand relative to everything else in your world.

So what is the great life? Only you can decide that. Everybody wants to be something they are not or have something they don't currently possess because they think that will get them the great life. These longings, coupled with the fact that most of us don't understand how to measure the great life, mean it is difficult to determine if we are already living the great life. *The 5 Keys to the Great Life* takes a reflective look at your current situation so you can decide whether you are already living the great life or if transformation is necessary. If you decide that transformation is necessary to live the great life, then this book shows you the methods for bridging the gap between where you are now and your great life.

While only you can decide what your great life looks like, years of research through practice and application shows us a great life is a balancing act of your personal universe, how you show up in it, and how you interact with it.

Jerry and Tomi come from a family of psychologists who operated within the framework of the ideas offered here. The concepts of the great life were used in our father's counseling practice, in Jerry's counseling practice, and in our sister Janie's practice, and in our own lives, for years. We know the principles we offer you work, because we see them in action.

As people begin to think about what their great life might look like, fear of change and transformation creep into their thoughts. Or, quite possibly, the inner critic rears its ugly head and tells you what you want is not possible. For this reason, Jerry and Tomi talk about reframing. We want to help you reframe your life. Reframing starts with recognizing that a great life is not a perfect life. Many of us spend too much time trying to be perfect and to have a perfect life. That is not the essence of The Great Life System. Instead, the essence of this system is finding the real, unique you and living authentically, not perfectly, within that frame.

The Great Life System provides tools, strategies, and resources for managing the ups and downs of life from a position of internal strength and power. Your strength and your power rest with your responses to the events in your universe and the level of responsibility you take for your own life. It is not a perfect life. Never has been. Never will be. But it can be a great life and that starts here.

Reframing your life includes dispelling one societal myth before moving to the 5 keys. Many times the response to the question, "What will make your life great?" is more money. While *The 5 Keys to the Great Life* is about wealth, it is more than financial wealth. Yes, money is important for the things for which it is important, but it is not the be all, end all. Look at the lives of Nelson Mandela or Mother Teresa, for example. Their accomplishments have held incredible value and meaning for them and others. They were able to change the world from a place other than a position of extreme wealth. Why is this so? Because money doesn't equal happiness. Elisabeth Kübler-Ross and David Kessler (2003) offer these thoughts on money and happiness:

> Our real power is not derived from our positions in life, a hefty bank account, or an impressive career. Instead, it is the expression of that authenticity inside of us, our strength, integrity, and grace externalized. We don't realize that each of us has the power of the universe within us....
>
> We tend to equate wealth with power, and we believe that money can buy happiness. Yet it is a sad day for many when they finally have that money but realize that they're not happy. Just as many rich people commit suicide as those who have not accumulated riches. Sigmund Freud once said that given a choice of treating rich or poor patients, he would

always choose the rich because they no longer think all their problems will be solved with money. (pp. 96-97)

Going in search of money isn't the answer. Go in search of your authentic self and the abundance will follow.

Jerry has his own personal example of how searching for the money does not always make you happy. Jerry was an executive with a government agency. He was paid a great salary for his work, but he was absolutely miserable. Plus, the job was costing him his good health. He became a stroke victim waiting to fall. His treating physician kept saying "Go pick out your coffin." Even though Jerry knew his health was compromised by his stress levels at work, he couldn't let go of the salary and status his position afforded. Jerry's cardiologist also told him to quit his job. Instead, Jerry asked for another doctor. The cardiologist told Jerry that the next person he was going to see was the mortician if he didn't quit his job. Jerry's 5Fs had gotten out of balance with finance being a primary focus. When Jerry heard the mortician comment, he then reassessed the 5Fs to find out what would allow him to realign himself with the great life on *this side* of death, or he was going to be living the great life on *the other side*.

Jerry quit his job. His wife quit her job. They sold their house and moved to a cabin in the mountains with no electricity and no water. Their television receives only two stations and they have to drive down the mountain for Internet service. Doesn't sound like the great life, does it? Well, it is. Jerry, Janice, and their two children, Nathan and Emily, live the adventure of a lifetime. They co-exist with the elk, the moose, the deer, the cougars, and one black bear. How many of us get to be that close to nature? The hot springs are about four miles away from Jerry's cabin so a regular dip in the hot pools stays on his calendar. Many people pay thousands of dollars for a vacation to do what Jerry and his family do every day. So, yes, this is the great life for Jerry and his family. The message here is that the great life isn't all about the money when it costs you the great life in other dimensions. For Jerry, the money wasn't worth the price of his health.

The great life is about letting go of the past. It is about understanding exactly where we are in this moment, and having a firm idea of where we want to go. It is about breaking the gridlock in our lives. What is meant by breaking the gridlock? Lama Surya Das (2000) provides an apt description of this process in *Awakening to the Sacred*: "We're all covered with layers and layers of encrusted barnacles, sediment, bits of seaweed, and odds and ends from our karmic scrap heap. These need to be chipped off a little at a time" (p. 36). With *The 5 Keys to the Great Life* you can start the chipping off process! We hear your thoughts at this exact moment: "Why do I need to chip off anything?" You don't have to. We aren't here to change you; we are here to hold a mirror up to ask your reflection this one question, "Do I like the way my life is right now, this very moment?" If the answer is no, then you can't keep doing the same thing if you want the great life. As Kübler-Ross (2003) stated in *Life Lessons*, the chipping away process is important, as it "will allow us all to be brilliant in one way or another, depending on our own gifts" (p. 35).

Albert Einstein defined insanity as doing the same thing over and over and expecting different results. Are you doing the same thing day-in and day-out yet expecting different results? As Lama Surya Das (2000) observed "We insist on doing things our own way, even if that way has already failed dozens of times" (p. 40). Or better yet, as Sandra Anne Taylor (2007) commented in *Quantum Success*, "If you change nothing, nothing will change" (p. 62). Having said that, we must reiterate we aren't here to change you; we are here to help you learn to create what you really want in life and to grow in the direction that brings you a great life. The ability to create originates with the ability to acknowledge where you are in this moment and take responsibility for that, whether or not you like where you are. As Kübler-Ross (2003) observed, "The grandest kind of perfection of who we are includes being honest about our dark sides, our imperfections" (p. 37).

John Maxwell was recently voted the number one leadership guru in the world by Leadership Gurus. Some of his observations about human nature from his book, *Leadership Gold*, help to further set the direction as we introduce The Great Life System. While Maxwell (2008) makes his observations about leaders, they adapt easily to the individual looking for the great life. First, people *hardly ever* see themselves candidly. Second, it seems that the human equation includes the aptitude for sizing up everyone on the planet but ourselves. Third, if you aren't able to see yourself as you really are, you can't appreciate where your own challenges rest—and if you are not able to recognize these difficulties, you can't lead yourself effectively to the great life! Fourth, it is imperative that we learn how to get out of our own way. Fifth, patience is required because few things in life arrive as fast as we want them to. "There is no such thing as instant greatness or instant maturity. We are used to instant oatmeal, instant coffee, and microwave popcorn" (Maxwell, 2008, p.15). Recognizing that a great life doesn't happen overnight is important. Microwave lives don't have staying-power. Instead, the great life is more of a crock-pot proposition. Getting to the great life takes time and effort, but you can do it, and it is worth it. Finally, as you take on the work of your great life, "If you worry about what other people think of you, it's because you have more confidence in their opinion than you have in your own" (Maxwell, 2008, p. 37).

As Maxwell (2008) set forth his observations, he offered two relevant quotes that drive home feelings that are a part of doing the work of your great life. The first quote is from Aldous Huxley: "You shall know the truth and the truth shall make you mad" (2008, p. 37). As you work through the tools, strategies, and resources offered in this book, so many of your habits and traits will come into focus. There will be many things to love about you. There will be some things that aren't loveable. And those things will make you mad. This is good! Seeing all of you is an important part of the acceptance process which is mandatory for the great life.

The second quote is from Judith Bardwick, and it serves well as an exclamation point to Maxwell's (2008) observations: "Real confidence comes from knowing and accepting yourself—your strengths and your limitations—in contrast to depending on affirmation from others" (p. 37). The great life is about accepting yourself and all that you are, or are not, in this moment, and moving forward from there. So, if you want to keep living the same life, do the same thing. If you want to live the great life, then start examining your karmic scrap heap.

Even though you are not aware of it, you are already operating within The Great Life System. It is just like gravity. Even though you can't see it, all of its principles are in play, every day, in every aspect of your life. The reason the system may not be working for you is your awareness of the structure, the playing field, and the rules is limited. Just as with gravity, unless you are a scientist, you don't try to understand its operation. You trust that it works without understanding it. We have applied the same philosophy to our personal lives for time immemorial: we don't need to understand the operation of our personal universe—*wing it* and see what happens. We jump into the boat of life without paddle or preserver and wait for the waters to rush at us. Unfortunately, that method no longer works.

One purpose of this book is to allow you to gain control of your life by bringing the operating system of your personal universe into your awareness. By seeing the structures dominating your life, you learn to recognize the forces at play in your life and see how to leverage them so that you can create your own great life. When you understand how gravity works, you can leverage its principles to make your life easier. For instance, traveling to space was out of the question until man removed the limitation of gravity. Once scientists understood how much force it took to break free of the constraints of gravity, traveling to the moon was no longer outside the realm of possibilities. Once you understand the principles that influence your universe, the great life is no longer outside the realm of possibilities. But, this book is only an opening, an invitation to test the 5 keys in your own life. Also, creating your own great life is an intensely personal process. While we offer the structure here, *you* must fill in the process.

When we talk about The Great Life System, we are talking about a structure. "The structure of anything refers to its fundamental parts and how those individual elements function in relation to each other and in relation to the whole" (Fritz, 1989, p. 6). The structure of The Great Life System involves the following:

1. The five keys of the system.

2. The six dimensions of the system.

3. The structural conflicts that can limit performance within the system.

4. Replacement strategies for improving performance.

In other words, we explain the fundamental parts of the System and how those individual elements function in relation to each other and in relation to the whole.

There is both an *art* and a *practice* to achieving the great life. It is an art, because sometimes we need to make a choice and let the process unfold. We have no influence over the process; our only option is the choice. It is a practice, because there are certain structured disciplines we can follow that will help us achieve the great life much faster. The Great Life System intermingles these arts and practices in such a way that finding a great life is possible for anyone, anywhere.

It does not matter what your beliefs about the world are. The principles of anything—any philosophy, religion, life strategy, therapy modality, behavioral modification theory, professional coaching strategy—can be dropped into the structure we discuss in this book. Because any life approach or practice will fit, we don't dedicate a lot of space to the practices of the different components of each dimension. Many books are available on a variety of the practices and strategies referenced here. For this reason, in *The 5 Keys to the Great Life* we primarily offer the system that allows you to view and implement these other works with more clarity and more understanding of their significance and impact on your life.

Understanding how you operate within the system allows you to determine if growth and transformation are necessary to enhance your performance. But it will be your choice and the whole process will be intensely personal to you.

There is so much more to living in this world then we let ourselves experience.

As you read this book, we suggest you keep in mind Larry Winget's (2009) principles from *People Are Idiots and I Can Prove It*:

- Your life is your own damn fault.

- Take responsibility for it.

- Learn what you need to do to fix it.

- Take action on what you've learned.

- Enjoy the results. (p. 8)

We want you to enjoy the great life and you can, by following the keys outlined in this book. It is worth it, and you can do it. So get ready because your great life is waiting!

Chapter 2

Key 1: Know the System

Structure determines behavior.
—Robert Fritz

Most of us aim for the wrong mark in the self-improvement arena. We universally believe behavior modification will solve all of our problems—improve our behavior, improve our lives. All it takes is will power, right? Wrong. In trying to alter the behavior that arises from the structure we live in, rather than trying to understand and transform the structure we live in, we are laying the track in the wrong direction. Because we live in a systems world, the exact opposite is true. The structure of the system in which we live dictates how we function; not vice versa. How can we begin to transform the structure that gives rise to our behavior when most of us have no clue what that underlying structure is? Systems thinking is the foundation of *The 5 Keys to the Great Life*, because it assists us with seeing through the complexity of our personal universe to that underlying structure. We aren't disregarding or ignoring the complexity of our personal universe. Rather, it means we are organizing that complexity into a logical system that offers clarity. This clarity allows us to see what is shaping and influencing our behavior in our personal universe. In this Chapter the first key of *Know the System* reveals to us the basics of the structure in which we all live.

Because systems thinking is fundamental to understanding the structure known as The Great Life System, a closer look at the tradition of this key is warranted. Systems thinking is the extension of systems theory, which has its ancestry in biology. Systems theory originated as a multi-disciplinary approach to seeing the structure that is the framework for any system. Senge (1994) broadened the application of systems theory, finding relevance in its application to the management field and renaming the theory "systems thinking."

According to Senge (1994) five unique disciplines come together in the management field to create the type of sustainable learning organization needed for the current tumultuous times: (a) systems thinking, (b) personal mastery,

(c) mental models, (d) building shared vision, and (e) team learning. Senge called these areas disciplines, because these are activities we must integrate into our lives—we must be disciplined about living the principles that make up each one. Senge showed disciplines are an integral requirement of thinking in systems. He saw systems thinking as the core discipline for his model for The Art & Practice of the Learning Organization. For this reason, *The 5 Keys to the Great Life* follows this approach but views the disciplines as keys.

Systems thinking is a multi-faceted concept: "At its broadest level, systems thinking encompasses a large and fairly amorphous body of methods, tools, and principles, all oriented to looking at the interrelatedness of forces, and seeing them as part of a common process" (Senge, Kleiner, Roberts, Ross, & Smith, 1994, p. 89). For Senge, the ultimate goal of systems thinking was to create a learning organization, the innovative corporate structure of the future. It is an organization where the participants understand their actions or inputs into the system create the problems or outputs of the system.

Also, systems thinking is considered a discipline for "seeing the 'structures' that underlie complex situations, and for discerning high from low leverage change" (Senge, 1994, p. 69). This "seeing of structures" involves a shift away from linear cause-and-effect thinking to circular, relationship thinking. As youngsters we are taught to break down problems under the pretext that this makes the complex more manageable. Unfortunately, according to Senge, we pay a price for this approach. It results in our inability to see the effects of our behaviors. We also don't have the feeling of being connected to a greater whole.

> We then try to "see the big picture," we try to reassemble the fragments in our minds, to list and organize all the pieces. But, as physicist David Bohm says, the task is futile—similar to trying to reassemble the fragments of a broken mirror to see a true reflection. Thus, after a while we give up trying to see the whole together. (Senge, 1994, p. 1)

Senge (1994) recognized the application of systems thinking was broad, observing that human endeavors are systems as well, because they are:

> Bound by invisible fabrics of interrelated actions, which often take years to fully play out their effects on each other. Since we are part of that lacework ourselves, it's doubly hard to see the whole pattern of change. Instead we tend to focus on snapshots of isolated parts of the system, and wonder why our deepest problems never seem to get solved. Systems thinking is a conceptual framework, a body of knowledge and tools that has been developed over the past fifty years, to make the full patterns clearer, and to help us see how to change them effectively. (p. 7)

There are many valuable principles to be borrowed from systems thinking to help us manage our current situation and lead us to the great life. According to Senge et al. (1994), it is this discipline that "helps us see how to change systems more effectively, and to act more in tune with the larger processes of the natural and economic world" (pp. 6-7). Most of us live piecemeal, managing personal crisis after personal crisis with little end in sight. We fail to view the day-to-day happenings of our lives in the larger scheme of our personal universe. This piecemeal approach limits our progress toward the great life in two ways. First, there is no clear understanding of how to change our lives more effectively. Second, we do not act in harmony with the whole of our personal universe. Systems thinking is the key to removing these limitations.

For Senge, while the product of systems thinking is a tool to create a learning organization, the end result is primarily about leverage. Leverage is seeing the pressure points for influence and change (Senge, 1994). The greatest benefit in systems thinking is the ability to see through the complexity of the structure to discern critical change points from non-critical change points.

In order to actualize systems thinking, we must change the basic way in which we look at our personal universe. People have been trained to think in a linear fashion. Thus, approaches to life issues have mainly been in a linear fashion:

However, systems thinking is a dynamic circle that reflects the interconnectedness of all the parts of the system. Diagramming a problem using systems thinking is dynamic, using a feedback loop like this:

The feedback loop reveals patterns of behavior created by the structure. It also reveals points of leverage. This process of using feedback loops to draw a picture of the story allows us to see the interrelationships among the parts and the mutual current of influence among the parts. These interrelationships and points of influence are what Jerry and his dad, Tom, saw in their counseling practices. It wasn't until Tomi came along with her systems thinking background that she and Jerry were able to peel back the layers of complexity from their own personal universes and those of their clients, to see the whole system. The Great Life System below in Figure 1 is what they saw staring back at them.

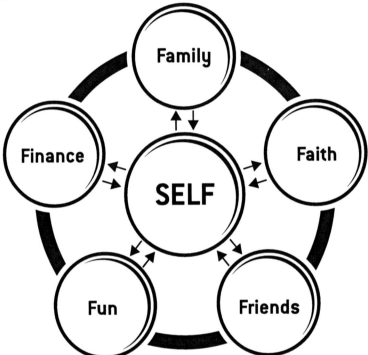

Figure 1. The Great Life System

To understand this System, we must do the following:

1. Learn about Self and the 5Fs (this is your personal universe).

2. Learn the language of the system (how we can influence it).

3. Learn strategies for accelerating performance within the system.

4. Learn about structural conflicts that are inherent in every system and how they may limit performance.

Your personal universe consists of the six dimensions of The Great Life System. Self is the center of The Great Life System, because in your personal universe, it is all about you! The other five dimensions revolve around you. The arrows that flow back and forth between Self and each of the other dimensions are our interactions with that dimension. The connections between each of the 5Fs are how those dimensions influence each other. The term interaction is a broad one and is meant to cover a lot of ground. It encompasses the other four keys: *Know the Language, Know the Mental Models, How to Use the Looking Glass,* and *How to Coach the Team.* We cover these keys to a great life in the remaining chapters.

Self

Self is the center of The Great Life System and it is You. It represents all the life experiences, beliefs, habits, attitudes, and behaviors that make up You. It is the image you hold of yourself, including concepts like self-image, self-worth, self-confidence, self-esteem, self-identity, self-centered, and selfishness. It includes your physical health, too.

Family

As used in The Great Life System, the term Family includes any person you consider a relative. Family is different from Friends as we can select Friends, but we don't get to select Family (except your spouse, unless you are in a compulsory marriage).

Faith

In The Great Life System, Faith represents your collective set of beliefs that influence your actions. These beliefs are built around social norms, assumed universal laws, religion, values, and your upbringing. These beliefs are called Mental Models. Everyone has these Mental Models, but most of us are not aware of them or the force they exert in our lives. The key of *Know the Mental Models* helps to bring these beliefs into focus.

Friends

In your personal universe, a Friend is an acquaintance you don't consider a relative but is still in your regular sphere of influence and with whom you like to spend time. Jerry and Tomi's dad, Tom, used to tell the family that they are who they hang out with. Tom always encouraged the family to associate with the right people. In fact, he used a metaphor to get this point across: "If you hang out in the barnyard long enough, you will step into a pile of manure."

Finances

In The Great Life System, Finances represents more than just money. It is about the abundance in your life at different levels. Finances mean career wealth, economic wealth, and impact wealth. Career wealth is your level of job satisfaction, including insurance like health and disability insurance, career satisfaction, and salary satisfaction. Economic wealth represents your net worth, including items like savings, income, valuables, investments, and retirement plans. Impact wealth means time or money. It is the ability to donate your time or your money to organizations of your choice, including your church.

Fun

As used in *The 5 Keys to the Great Life*, Fun means those activities you engage in for rest and relaxation including hobbies and interests, such as reading, playing on the computer, surfing the web, going to a concert, visiting a museum, painting, playing electronic games, bowling, hiking, boating, bike riding, swimming, watching movies, cooking, hunting, skiing, and the like. For the adults in the group, Fun also includes sex and intimacy. Of course, Fun is about the laughter in your life.

Every person or thing in your life can be associated with one of these six dimensions. For instance, you're unhappy at your job. That concern is about career wealth and falls within the parameters of the Finance dimension. Your really great relationship with your half-brother is in the Family dimension. You like to gamble, drink, dance, and party. All of those items crop up in the Fun dimension. If for some reason you don't like who you are, that places your concern in the Self dimension. The happier and more fulfilled you are in each dimension, the more outward your universe expands. However, expansion can be healthy and unhealthy. The goal is to engage in healthy expansion of your universe to increase the greatness of your life.

Before we discuss the other 4 keys to the great life, let's profile your current situation using The Great Life Profile set forth in Figure 2. If you want a printable copy of The Great Life Profile, then visit www.5greatkeys.com to complete an electronic version.

DIRECTIONS: This Profile contains a set of questions for each of the six dimensions of The Great Life System that represent your personal universe. It is a way of graphically displaying your life as it is in this moment (current reality). As you read each of the statements in the Profile, rank how you feel about that statement on a scale from 1 (Highly Disagree) to 10 (Highly Agree). Please be candid in your responses. Add your score at the bottom of each section to obtain a subtotal.

Section 1: Self

SELF: Represents all the life experiences, beliefs, habits, attitudes and behaviors that make up You. It is the image you hold of yourself and includes concepts like self-image, self-worth, self-confidence, self-esteem, self-identity, self-centered, and selfishness. It also encompasses your health.

	Score of 1-10
I am satisfied with myself.	
I feel I have a number of unique qualities and skills.	
I make the difficult decisions that need to be made.	
I have a positive attitude toward myself and life.	
I regularly engage in activities that help me grow.	
I learn from my mistakes.	
I take responsibility for my physical health and well being.	
I am in good health.	
I take responsibility for things I have done.	
I am the appropriate weight for my height.	
I eat a well balanced diet.	
I am courageous.	
There is no one that I need to forgive.	
I am able to focus clearly on the tasks in my life.	
I am in control of my happiness.	
I stop and think things over before doing them.	
I am self confident.	
I have a plan for my life.	
I am organized.	
I am good at tolerating frustration.	
Subtotal	

Section 2: Family

FAMILY: Includes any person you consider a relative. Family is different from Friends as we can select Friends but we don't get to select Family (except your spouse unless you are in a compulsory marriage).

	Score of 1-10
I am satisfied with the amount of time I spend with my family.	
I participate in family activities.	
I put extra effort into making sure my family's needs are met.	
I have created the experience of family in my life with those close to me.	
I create loving relationships.	
I am free from past resentments with my family members.	
I am proud of what my family represents.	
I show love and affection to my family members.	
I am satisfied with the level of support I receive from my family.	
I feel nothing is hidden or withheld in my relationships with family members.	
I put my family issues as a top priority.	
I am in tune with my family's feelings.	
I openly discuss family issues.	
I enjoy laughing and having fun with my family.	
I turn to my family for advice.	
I am satisfied with the level of commitment my family provides.	
I am satisfied with the role I play and the level of contribution I have in my family.	
I fit into my family.	
I say the things that need to be said to family members with compassion and kindness.	
My family makes me feel comfortable.	
Subtotal	

Section 3: Faith

FAITH: Represents your collective set of beliefs that influence your actions. These beliefs are built around social norms, universal law, religion, values and your upbringing.

	Score of 1-10
I participate in prayer, reflection, meditation, or worship.	
I am satisfied with the time I spend in prayer, reflection, meditation, or worship.	
I put forth extra effort into my faith.	
I experience harmony in my life because of my faith.	
I am a spiritual or religious person.	
My faith allows me to be free from past resentments.	
I am proud of my faith.	
I believe there is some real purpose for my life.	
I am comforted by my spiritual or religious beliefs.	
My faith supports the direction my life is taking.	
I put my faith as a top priority.	
I am in tune with my belief system.	
I openly discuss issues about my faith with others.	
I am serious about my faith.	
I turn to my prayer, reflection, mediation, or worship for advice on issues.	
I am satisfied with the level of participation I have in my faith.	
I am satisfied with the role I play and the level of contribution I have in my faith.	
I follow through on things I believe in.	
My faith gives me a sense of fulfillment.	
My faith sustains me no matter what situations occur.	
Subtotal	

Section 4: Friends

FRIENDS: An acquaintance you don't consider a relative but is still in your regular sphere of influence and with whom you like to spend time.

	Score of 1-10
I participate in activities with my friends.	
I am a good friend and I make myself available.	
I am satisfied with the amount of time I spend with my friends.	
I have truthful and trusting relationships with my friends.	
I create new friendships.	
I am free from past resentments with my friends.	
I am proud of my friends and what they represent.	
I show care and compassion for my friends.	
I am satisfied with the level of support I receive from my friends.	
I feel nothing is hidden or withheld in my friendships.	
I put my friends' issues as a top priority.	
I am in tune with my friend's feelings.	
I say the things that need to be said to my friends with compassion and kindness.	
I enjoy laughing and having fun with my friends.	
I turn to my friends for advice.	
I am satisfied with the number of friends I have.	
I have a lot in common with my friends.	
I feel like my friends accept and respect my opinions.	
My friends like to explore new opportunities.	
My friends make me feel comfortable.	
Subtotal	

Section 5: Finances

FINANCES: Includes career wealth, economic wealth and impact wealth. Career wealth is your level of job satisfaction, including insurance like health and disability insurance, career satisfaction and salary satisfaction. Economic wealth represents your net worth, including items like savings, income, valuables, investments and retirement plans. Impact wealth means time or money. It is the ability to donate your time or your money to organizations of your choice, including your church.

	Score of 1-10
I have enough money for the important things I need.	
I have enough money for the things I want.	
I am willing to put extra effort into making money.	
I am satisfied with my job.	
I am satisfied with my salary.	
I have enough insurance.	
I am proud of where I work.	
I like the people where I work.	
I am satisfied with the level of support I receive from my coworkers.	
I feel nothing is hidden or withheld in my relationships at work.	
I put work as a top priority.	
I enjoy laughing and having fun at work.	
I turn to my coworkers for advice.	
I am respected at work.	
I am willing to seek new career opportunities.	
I do not worry about money issues.	
I am satisfied with the amount of time or money I donate to charities.	
I am financially stable.	
My money, financial affairs, and records are well managed.	
My work makes me feel comfortable.	
Subtotal	

Section 6: Fun

FUN: Those activities you engage in for rest and relaxation including hobbies and interests. Examples include reading, playing on the computer, surfing the web, going to a concert, visiting a museum, painting, playing electronic games, bowling, hiking, boating, bike riding, swimming, watching movies, cooking, hunting, skiing, and the like. For the adults in the group, Fun also includes intimacy. Finally, Fun is about the laughter in your life.

	Score of 1-10
I participate in recreational activities.	
I am satisfied with the recreational activities I currently participate in.	
I am satisfied with the amount of time I take for fun, leisure, and relaxation.	
I use my leisure time well and enjoy it.	
I create fun for myself and others.	
I make fun of myself.	
I have fun.	
I have a sense of freedom and adventure in my life.	
I am satisfied with the activities I have chosen for fun, leisure, and relaxation.	
I know how to relax and have fun.	
I put fun as a top priority.	
I can laugh at what happens to me.	
I participate in new and different activities.	
I enjoy laughing and having fun.	
I turn to fun to escape life's pressures.	
I am satisfied with the amount of time I spend laughing.	
I am able to set appropriate limits for my activities.	
I do something for fun and recreation on a regular basis.	
I like comedy, jokes, and funny events.	
My choices in fun make me feel comfortable.	
Subtotal	

Figure 2. The Great Life Profile

Summarize your scores by placing the subtotal from each dimension in the appropriate space in the table below in the subtotal column (also available in the downloadable version on the website):

Dimension/Life Area	Subtotal	Divide by 2	Total (plot this score on Figure 3)
Self		÷2	
Family		÷2	
Faith		÷2	
Friends		÷2	
Finances		÷2	
Fun		÷2	
		Subtotal	

Divide your subtotal by 2 to obtain a total score for each dimension. Take the total from each of the six dimensions and plot them on the graph in Figure 3 in the appropriate section and shade the area inward. See Figure 4 for an example of how the final Profile should look.

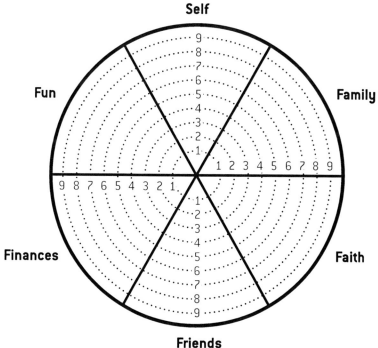

Figure 3.

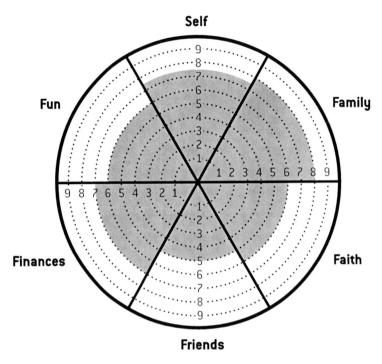

Figure 4.

Upon completion of the Profile, ask yourself this question: "Am I satisfied with my life?" Also, ask yourself, "Does my Profile reflect my idea of a great life?" If the answer is no, then keep reading, because your great life is waiting and the rest of this book will show you how to get there. If the answer is yes, congratulations! You should keep reading, too, as the information shared in the rest of this book will allow you to keep your momentum going. If that doesn't interest you, then you should immediately loan this book to a friend so he or she can find the great life.

The rest of this book examines ways you can expand outward those dimensions that you are not satisfied with. Of course, expansion needs to be in a healthy manner as opposed to an unhealthy manner.

Keep your Profile handy as you continue to read this book. We will revisit this Profile as you learn more about the other 4 keys to the great life.

In this Chapter we set the stage for why our old habits won't work in this new era. The idea is simple—old structures won't work in a new world. In fact those old structures don't support our success and actually create boundaries which hold us back from the great life. Because complexity and chaos often overwhelm us, we need new methods of operation in this fast-paced world. A primary method is understanding the function of structures. Jerry and Tomi examined their own and other's life experiences in order to more fully see the structure of the world in which we live. From these experiences, they developed The Great Life System. The remainder of this book takes you more deeply through this System so you can leverage its forces to create your great life.

Chapter 3

Key 2: Know the Language

If you don't design your own life plan, chances are you'll fall into someone else's plan. And guess what they have planned for you? Not much.
—*Jim Rohn*

The key of *Know the System* teaches that all things operate within a system. Even if we can't see the system, one is still at work. Equally so, all systems have rules or laws that govern their operation. For example, as we previously discussed, there is a rule book for how to operate in the system known as football. Each culture has laws to maintain order and to let people know how to operate in society. There are protocols for conducting medical research. There are grading scales in school. Just like those systems, The Great Life System has rules of operation. In order to be able to follow the rules, we first need to know what they are. In order to leverage the rules to our benefit and understand where points of influence are, we need to be able to speak the same language as the system; thus, this second key, *Know the Language*, builds upon the structure set forth in Chapter 2 by examining the rules of operation for the system, including points of influence and structural conflicts. Awareness and understanding of how to leverage operation of The Great Life System allows you to maximize the system's capabilities to quickly reach the great life.

Philosophers and scientists have sought the truisms of life and the universe for centuries, looking for a universal language of life, without overwhelming success. It seemed unlikely that Jerry and Tomi could find something for which others had searched for centuries. However, ignorance is bliss, sometimes. Like antsy novices, we jumped into worlds of information and research not always familiar to us. As Jerry and Tomi began to research the language of The Great Life System, they searched across many traditions from philosophy to physics. Even so, we had a guiding principle as we filtered through information: our search focused on finding the truth of the underlying principles of the universe's operation as we understand it today. We wanted to be able to point to scientific proof that the universe operates in a specific way. We wanted repeatable behaviors. We wanted evidence that when we do x, then y happens. This part of our quest took us to different places and across disciplines.

Philosophy appeared to be a likely place to start trying to find this *universal language*. The field of philosophy represents an attempt to find a unified theory that explains reality. From the Socratic Method to Kant's constructivist philosophy, traditional philosophers searched for a means to know the absolute truth. They understood there had to be some fixed, logical principles that governed reality. However, philosophy didn't offer Jerry and Tomi what they were looking for in the way of provable truths about the way the world operates; so, they turned to other disciplines.

The last part of the 20th century saw a resurgence of interest in universal truths from spiritual leaders, mystics, and new agers. Dr. Wayne Dyer, Dr. Doreen Virtue, and Deepak Chopra all wrote books about such truths. Based on this resurgence of interest, Jerry and Tomi's next research stop was to step back in time, approximately 5000 years to the ancient Chinese capital of Luoyang when Lao-tzu lived.

Lao-tzu was a prophet to whom the Tao Te Ching is attributed. The Tao Te Ching has survived for centuries, translated in almost every language and with thousands of versions in existence. So many versions exist because of the different ways in which the Chinese language can be interpreted. A fascinating modern interpretation of the Tao Te Ching is Dr. Dyer's version entitled *Change Your Thoughts, Change Your Life: Living the Wisdom of the Tao*. Dr. Dyer (2007) defined the Tao as: "the supreme reality, an all-pervasive Source of everything. The Tao never begins or ends, does nothing, and yet animates everything in the world of form and boundaries, which is called 'the world of the 10,000 things'" (p. xii). Scholars have proclaimed the *Tao* one of the most profound books in the development of world philosophy. The *Tao* was seen as the *all pervasive Source of everything*—that sounded like it could be the language of how The Great Life System operates. So, Jerry and Tomi took a closer look.

The *Tao* is comprised of 81 verses that act as guiding principles for life. To determine if the Tao was the language of The Great Life System, Jerry and Tomi studied some of these verses in depth. We randomly decided to take a closer look at the 33rd verse of "living self-mastery". Dr. Dyer interprets this verse to mean that attention should be aimed at understanding yourself instead of attributing fault to others. He believes that Lao-tzu is encouraging you to have:

> A Tao-oriented life focuses on understanding yourself, rather than on the thinking and behaviors of others. You shift from the acquisition of

information and the pursuit of status symbols to understanding and mastering yourself in all situations. Power over others is replaced with an inner strength that empowers you to behave from a wisdom that is inherently the Tao.

As you modify your thinking, your world will undergo pleasantly dramatic changes. For example, as you realize you are responsible for your reactions in any given moment, others will cease to have any power or control over you. Rather than worrying, *Why is that person behaving that way and making me feel so upset?* you can see the situation as an invitation to explore yourself from a new attitude of self-mastery...

It's important to bypass blame and even your desire to understand the other person; instead, focus on understanding *yourself*. By taking responsibility for how you choose to respond to anything or anyone, you're aligning yourself with the Tao. (Dyer, 2007, pp. 161-163)

Some of the guiding principles of the *Tao* intersect with the laws of the universe (another set of principles we examine later in this Chapter). Verse 19 of the *Tao* is interpreted as "Living without Attachment," which is considered a universal law. The *Tao* and the Universal Laws intersect at some points and the *Tao* offers words to live by, but for Jerry and Tomi the *Tao* didn't seem to provide the specific underpinnings needed to govern or to understand the interactions of our personal universes. For this reason, Jerry and Tomi pushed forward in time to ancient Egypt and the time of Hermes.

The ancient writings and teachings of Hermes became known as the Hermetic philosophy. However, these teachings were not captured in writing until 1908 when three anonymous Hermetic teachers published them in *The Kybalion*. Dr. Virtue (2006) offered a new interpretation of *The Kybalion* in her book *Divine Magic: The Seven Sacred Secrets of Manifestation*. Dr. Virtue highlights the seven sacred principles offered by Hermes, noting that following these principles allows one to maintain moods, thoughts and vibrations at high levels, resulting in enhanced relationships, finances and health, to name a few. Below is a list of these principles and a brief summary of their meaning:

1. Mentalism: "The All is Mind; The Universe is Mental."

2. Correspondence: "As above, so below; as below, so above."

3. Vibration: "Nothing rests; everything moves; everything vibrates."

4. Polarity: "Everything is Dual; everything has poles; everything has its pair of opposites; like and unlike are the same; opposites are identical in

nature, but different in degree; extremes meet; all truths are but half-truths; all paradoxes may be reconciled."

5. Rhythm: "Everything flows, out and in; everything has its tides; all things rise and fall; the pendulum-swing manifests in everything; the measure of the swing to the right is the measure of the swing to the left; rhythm compensates."

6. Cause and Effect: "Every Cause has its Effect; every Effect has its Cause; everything happens according to Law; Chance is but a name for Law not recognized; there are many planes of causation, but nothing escapes the Law."

7. Gender: "Gender is in everything; everything has its Masculine and Feminine Principles; Gender manifests on all planes." (Virtue, 2006, pp. 2-5)

While these maxims caused Jerry and Tomi to pause because they sounded somewhat based in science and possibly provable, the Hermetic principles still didn't feel like the language of The Great Life System. Possibly, Deepak Chopra's *The Seven Laws of Spiritual Success* would offer more.

Chopra (1994) wrote "Success in life could be defined as the continued expansion of happiness and the progressive realization of worthy goals. Success is the ability to fulfill your desires with effortless ease" (p. 2). This observation mirrored what Jerry and Tomi believed about the function of The Great Life System. The point of a great life is to expand your personal universe outward so you can receive and accommodate all the abundance possible in each dimension. That certainly sounded like "continued expansion of happiness and the progressive realization of worthy goals." Another point of a great life is that it should come with ease. That certainly sounded like "the ability to fulfill your desires with effortless ease." Based on these comments, Jerry and Tomi delved further into Chopra's seven laws.

As we examined the law of giving, the law of karma or cause and effect, the law of least effort, the law of intention and desire, the law of detachment, and the law of dharma or purpose in life, our nerves tingled a little bit and our hearts fluttered. These laws could possibly be the operating rules for The Great Life System. In addition to these seven laws, Chopra hinted at the existence of the quantum field and that it is nothing other than energy and information. He even wrote that, "The whole universe, in its essential nature, is the movement of energy and information" (Chopra, 1994, p. 68). Chopra was moving in the right direction but something was still missing from these seven laws and his explanations. While we couldn't explain why Chopra's seven laws didn't answer our question—other than our scientific minds remained unconvinced—it felt right to keep researching.

Our research would not have been complete without an examination of religious principles. Tommy Newberry's (2007) *Success is not an Accident* offers seven faith-based lessons for creating success in your life. His philosophy is that one must choose success, choose who you want to become, choose to write down compelling goals, choose to invest your time wisely, choose to get out of your own way, choose positive visualization and choose a maximum-energy lifestyle. Bible references are part of these seven lessons. However, science essentially played no role in the seven lessons he identified; so, we moved on.

Herbert Harris' (2007) *The Twelve Universal Laws of Success* is also faith-based. He uses the Bible "as a source of spiritual principle and as a textbook in universal law" (Harris, 2007, p. 23). He uses biblical verses to help explain his 12 laws: the law of thought, the law of change, the law of vision, the law of command, the law of magnetism, the law of focus, the law of action, the law of value, the law of relationships, the law of supply, the law of persistence, and the law of truth. These laws sounded like universal truths. However, they, too, were missing the underlying science connection we felt was needed for The Great Life System.

It was at this point that Jerry and Tomi decided to revise their hypothesis. Why were we not satisfied to rest with spirituality, eastern traditions, or religion as the language of The Great Life System? We decided it is important to have quantifiable rules of engagement for the System in order to be able to see points of leverage. We wanted to be able to back up the workings of the System with science, because sometimes people need concrete evidence and application. Our initial research seemed focused in the wrong area. For these reasons, we shifted our research hypothesis from "finding the truth of the underlying principles of the operation of the universe as we understand it today", to "finding the *scientific* truth of the universe as we know it today." That shift immediately pushed us toward physics, Einstein, and his belief that everything is energy.

Einstein's research convinced Jerry and Tomi that physics may hold the answer to cracking the language code for The Great Life System. Einstein's general theory of relativity states that matter and energy actually mold the shape of space and flow of time. Another of Einstein's theories proposed that space and time and matter and energy are all linked together in the most intimate embrace. Based on the research of Einstein, Jerry and Tomi began to see energy might be the basis for the language of The Great Life System. While Einstein's theories pointed us in a certain direction scientifically, his theories didn't provide definitive answers.

Jerry and Tomi deduced that if everything is energy that meant every dimension in The Great Life System was also energy. Jerry and Tomi firmly believed that if they could understand how energy behaves and what influences energy, those maxims would be the rules of operation for The Great Life System. In other words, if we know the rules of operation, we can exert our influence over them to create the great life. Jerry and Tomi extended their research to include authors who attempted to link success and physics.

We came across several authors who wrote about that connection. For instance, in Brenda Anderson's (2006) *Playing the Quantum Field*, she noted that:

> Science is on the verge of proving that everything is dynamic and connected. What was once considered the New Age fringe thinking of renegade physicists has been embraced by more and more people as a probability. This new worldview is reflected in key scientific discoveries, kicked off by Einstein a century ago, and is becoming so widely accepted that it was celebrated by the World Year of Physics in 2005. The quantum field is showing itself up close and personal for increasing numbers of us. (p. 5)

Anderson also confirmed Jerry and Tomi's belief that if we can just understand the language of the universe, we would be able to harness its power to create the great life. She said that

> What we are really talking about with the quantum field is possibility. Think of the quantum field as all possibility and potential, which you can consciously access—if you know how. Anyone who studies quantum physics knows that your thoughts connect you to this field of possibility. (Anderson, 2006, p. 7)

However, for Jerry and Tomi, Anderson's theories still did not have that all-inclusive feel of being the language of the universe.

In Sandra Anne Taylor's (2007) *Quantum Success*, she makes some of the same connections as Anderson. The introduction to her book quickly identified the relationship between physics and the possibilities we are capable of by writing, "In quantum physics, the uncertainty theory reveals that you live in a state of unending possibilities that are of your own making" (Taylor, 2007, p. x). She even connects the self to energy, stating, "Your soul is connected to the powerhouse that charges all of creation, and it's time to open yourself to that Universal current—that pulsating energy that directs your destiny" (pp. xiv-xv). Taylor offers some important points to ponder. Yet, we felt like we were playing the children's game of Huckle Buckle Beanstalk in which we kept getting warmer and warmer but we weren't there yet. But what we saw of quantum physics led us to believe this field is focused on identifying and understanding the unseen forces at work in the universe. We had the sense we were on the right track.

In turning to a purely scientific approach, Jerry and Tomi went to Brian Greene's (2005) *The Elegant Universe*. Greene provides the reader with an overview of how far the field of physics has come in understanding the fundamental laws of the universe. While string theory is fascinating, *The Elegant Universe* didn't offer principles that converted to a practical language of the universe.

Just when frustrations rose, because we worried that we wouldn't find the answer, Tomi remembered reading a book about a science-based explanation of how the universe operates. That book was Gregg Braden's (2007) *The Divine Matrix*. Braden, formerly an aerospace computer systems designer, describes his research into the language of the universe as blending the best science available. Jerry and Tomi appreciated Braden's multi-disciplinary approach, which crossed the conventional boundaries of science, history, and religion. After re-reading Braden's material, Jerry and Tomi knew at last *The Divine Matrix* was the foundation for the language of The Great Life System. If we understand and use Braden's ideas, which include four discoveries and 20 keys about energy and physics for The Great Life System, we gain the power to create the great life we so richly deserve.

Braden (2007) describes four discoveries related to the field of energy:

Just as all life is built from the four chemical bases that create our DNA, the universe appears to be founded upon four characteristics of the Divine Matrix that make things work in the way they do. The key to tapping the power of the Matrix lies in our ability to embrace the four landmark discoveries that link it to our lives in an unprecedented way:

Discovery 1: There is a field of energy that connects all of creation.

Discovery 2: This field plays the role of a container, a bridge, and a mirror for the beliefs within us.

Discovery 3: The field is nonlocal and holographic. Every part of it is connected to every other, and each piece mirrors the whole on a smaller scale.

Discovery 4: We communicate with the field through the language of emotion.

It's our power to recognize and apply these realities that determine everything from our healing to the success of our relationships and careers. (p. xxi)

Braden explains the significance of understanding how energy operates by observing that "The key to mastering this place of pure energy is to know that it exists, to understand how it works, and finally to speak the language that it recognizes. All things become available to us as the architects of reality in this place…" (2007, p. 4). And, this place, where Braden says the world begins, is the Divine Matrix.

Braden expands the four landmark discoveries into 20 keys of conscious creation. These keys work in concert to offer us the scientific basis for the language for which we so desperately searched. This language allows us to see the interrelationships among the parts of our personal universe, including the mutual current of influence among those parts. Here are Braden's 20 Keys:

- Key 1: The Divine Matrix is the *container* that holds the universe, the *bridge* between all things, and the *mirror* that shows us what we have created.

- Key 2: Everything in our world is connected to everything else.

- Key 3: To tap the force of the universe itself, we must see ourselves as *part* of the world rather than *separate from* it.

- Key 4: Once something is joined, *it is always connected*, whether it remains physically linked or not.

- Key 5: The act of focusing our consciousness is an act of creation. Consciousness creates!

- Key 6: We have all the power we need to create all the changes we choose!

- Key 7: The focus of our awareness becomes the reality of our world.

- Key 8: To simply *say* that we choose a new reality is not enough!

- Key 9: Feeling is the language that "speaks" to the Divine Matrix. Feel as though your goal is accomplished and your prayer is already answered.

- Key 10: Not just any feeling will do. The ones that create must be without ego and judgment.

- Key 11: We must *become* in our lives the things that we choose to *experience* as our world.

- Key 12: We are not bound by the laws of physics as we know them today.

- Key 13: In a holographic "something," every piece of the something mirrors the whole something.

- Key 14: The universally connected hologram of consciousness promises that the instant we create our good wishes and prayers, they are already received at their destination.

- Key 15: Through the hologram of consciousness, a little change in our lives is mirrored everywhere in our world.

- Key 16: The minimum number of people required to "jump-start" a change in consciousness is $\sqrt{1\%}$ of a population.

- Key 17: The Divine Matrix serves as the mirror in our world of the relationships that we create in our beliefs.

- Key 18: The root of our "negative" experiences may be reduced to one of three universal fears (or a combination of them): abandonment, low self-worth, or lack of trust.

- Key 19: Our true beliefs are mirrored in our most intimate relationships.

- Key 20: We must become in our lives the very things that we choose to experience in our world. (pp. 208-209)

In order to leverage the power of energy or to be able to influence it in ways which help us create the great life, these discoveries and keys need to be translated into action. Only then can we begin to influence our lives in profound ways.

Based on their research, Jerry and Tomi were able to discern the following scientific truths about the universe as we know it today:

> We are all connected by the flow of energy and matter. If you know how energy behaves, you have the knowledge and power to create your universe just as you desire it. And, your ability to do so is limitless.

Using these truths, we now have the ability to discern what behaviors attract to us all that we desire. In other words, we are one step closer to unlocking the secrets to the great life.

Braden's first key is the most essential and holds important information for understanding operation of The Great Life System. This key emphasizes the role of the Divine Matrix as the container, bridge and mirror. Let's put some definition around *container*, *bridge*, and *mirror* so we can understand their importance to The Great Life System. When we reference a container, we mean what gently holds and envelops all of our universe. Energy particles are everywhere. Because they are omnipresent, they make up the container that holds the six dimensions of The Great Life System. Moreover, when we take action on something, we set energy in motion among the Self and the 5Fs. This energy in motion (the action) is the bridge between Self and the other five dimensions. All energy in motion moves at a certain pace or frequency. When we send out energy in the form of an action, it is moving at a certain pace and is going to attract like energy, meaning energy moving at the same pace. So if we send out a positive vibration, a positive vibration will be attracted in response. Thus, the response we receive then mirrors what we sent out into the universe; thus, the energy of the Divine Matrix acts as the container, the bridge, and the mirror of the universe. With this information, we can update The Great Life System to reflect the role and impact of the Divine Matrix. See Figure 5 for the revised system.

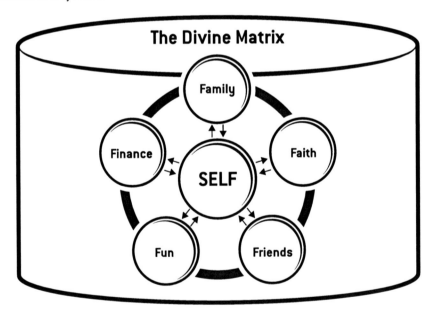

Figure 5. The Great Life System Revised

Now, we can turn to examining the implications of the container, bridge, and mirror on the language of The Great Life System. First, we must live and behave in a manner consistent with the belief that all people and all things are connected. This means recognizing that energy is the container in which we live and energy is the bridge between Self and the other five dimensions of your personal universe. Energy is projected outward by the Self in the form of thoughts and feelings. These thoughts and feelings result in actions that are a bridge to the other dimensions. What we send out immediately as thoughts, feelings, and actions impacts our whole universe.

As Braden's keys explain, we operate in a hologram that instantly delivers to the whole universe and mirrors back to us all that we do. Whatever we do to someone or something, we really are doing to ourselves; hence, the rule of "First, do no harm". We should honor and respect all people and all things. If we don't, we aren't respecting ourselves, either. Tomi tells her children to respect all people as everyone has something to offer; we simply may not be able to see it in this moment. She believes all people are great, but they may not have found their greatness, yet. Just because we can't see the greatness doesn't mean it isn't there. So, honor the greatness in all people whether you witness it or not.

Since everything is connected, the speed of the movement of the energy particles or the frequency of vibration of the energy particles that make up your Self is how you dictate what you attract in your life. Like objects move at like speeds or frequencies. So, whatever frequency or vibration you project outward is what you get back. It works just like a boomerang—throw something out into the universe and it comes back to you. Sandra Anne Taylor's (2007) *Quantum Success* offers a great analogy of how this works:

> We can only attract the same kind of energy that we put out about ourselves…

> Each of us is like a little radio station, constantly broadcasting signals about our self and our life. The people and situations that match those signals are the ones that will tune in to us and be drawn into our life experience. (p. 10)

What is often identified as *chemistry* is more of a tone, a corresponding of signals and individual vibrations (Taylor, 2007). What determines your level of vibration in the universe is your attitude and your self-talk. Know what you are broadcasting over the universal airwaves, because that is what mirrors back to you. Braden's (2007) keys validate so many of the universal or spiritual laws, such as the law of vibration and the law of attraction that others have written about for years. Now, we can understand these laws in a scientific context.

To have a great life, a positive attitude and positive self talk are mandatory. By thinking positively, you set your body at a positive vibration so it attracts people and things with a similar vibration, or like positive things. A variety of books are available on positive attitudes, creating positive energy for yourself and changing how your mind works. Find any one of those books which speak to you and drop those practices in right here, and you have already begun practicing some of the language of The Great Life System.

Wayne Cordeiro (2001), in *Attitudes That Attract Success: You Are Only One Attitude Away From A Great Life*, offers a useful way to view The Great Life System with a positive attitude:

> What is important is not the current state of your family, your problems, who your boss is or how much money you make. What is important is your attitude toward family, toward problems, toward authority and toward money. Attitude makes all the difference in the world! (p. 16-17)

Thinking positively is only part of the language. Silencing the inner critic is also essential. The inner critic is that voice inside your head that rarely has anything nice to say to you. It is easy to call up. If you want to hear it, look in the mirror and say the statements below to yourself. After you say each sentence, pause to hear what the inner critic says back:

1. I am so beautiful/handsome!

2. I love my body!

3. I am smart!

4. I am going to write a bestseller.

When Tomi used to say these things to herself, the inner critic answered as follows:

1. I am so beautiful/handsome!

   Inner critic response: *No you are not. Your nose is too big and you hair is awful.*

2. I love my body!

   Inner critic response: *You are kidding, right? You are still carrying around all that weight you gained with your last child. Are you ever going to lose that?*

3. I am smart!

   Inner critic response: *Maybe you are but there is always someone smarter.*

4. I am going to write a bestseller.

Inner critic response: You are such a loser. Your writing is awful. Ain't gonna happen!

Ouch! We are so mean to ourselves. We wouldn't be that mean or ugly to a family member or a friend so why should we be that way to ourselves? It is important to be your own best friend and to love yourself completely. When you hear these negative comments in your head, immediately stop. Tell yourself positive things. Let your mind know you hear it. For instance, when you hear something like, "Your nose is too big and you hair is awful.," respond with a positive comment such as, "I hear you but I have a great smile that lights up my whole face. My blue eyes are beautiful and people compliment me on these regularly." Find something positive to think about and don't let the conversation in your head end with a negative comment. Always end on a positive comment.

Another part of the language is acting as if. We must feel as though what we want exists already so that the holograph of the Divine Matrix will mirror that same scenario back to us. Visualizing the successful outcome as already having taken place and feeling the emotion of that outcome is an excellent way to achieve this. Elite athletes are great at visualizing and feeling triumph before a competition. (See Ron Sirak, Pia Nilsson and Lynn Marriott's *The Game Before The Game: The Perfect 30-Minute Practice* (2007) or Ivan Misner and Dan Morgan's *Masters of Success* (2004).) This same practice is the one to employ in your everyday life about everything you want. Another way to implement this part of the language is by making collages, story boards, meditating, or praying.

One way Tomi speaks this part of the language is each morning before rising, she sees the day playing out in her head. She sees the day unfolding as a great one and that everything she wants to accomplish is already done. She also has a list of mantras she runs through:

> Thank you for this beautiful day, my great husband, my great kids, my great job, my great house, and my great life. Please hold my family in the palm of your hand today, protecting them from head to toe. May all people have safe passage today as they go about their daily routines. As I go about my business today, I am a client magnet, a money magnet, and money comes to me easily and frequently. I have the mind of a millionaire. I ask for forgiveness and forgive all. May judgments and criticisms elude me today. Already done and so it is.

Again, there are many authors who have written excellent books on visualization, goal setting, and faking it until you make it. For this reason, it makes no sense to write about those techniques here. We reiterate our encouragement to go to your favorite bookstore and find a book on this topic that speaks to you. Learn those practices that fit your lifestyle and you add another part of the language of The Great Life System into your life. Tomi found help in this department while reading how to create your own personal prayer book in Lama Surya Das' (2000) *Awakening to the Sacred: Creating a Personal Spiritual Life*. Daily Devotionals also work. If you are unsure where to start, check out Richard Webster's (2006) *Creative Visualization for Beginners* or Shari Just and Carolyn Flynn's (2005) *Complete Idiot's Guide to Creative Visualization*.

Another piece of the language for The Great Life System derives from the fact that the Divine Matrix is a mirror. Thus, everything that happens to us is a reflection of what we created for ourselves. We can use this information to provide two more parts of the language. First, everything that is happening in our lives is a reflection of what we believe about ourselves. In order to see this reflection, we suggest you complete the Belief Assessment tool in Figure 6, by asking yourself these three questions about each of the six dimensions:

1. "What does the mirror show me about what I have created in this dimension?"

2. "What does that mean I believe about myself in this dimension?"

3. "What am I pretending not to know about myself in this dimension?"

This is a great place to begin to use the AWE method: Analyze, Write, and Explain. For each dimension, as you ask the questions, analyze your answers, write about your answers, and then explain your findings to a friend or partner to see if your conclusions make sense.

Dimension	What does the mirror show me about what I have created in this dimension?	What does that mean I believe about myself in this dimension?	What am I pretending not to know about myself in this dimension?
Self			
Family			
Faith			
Friends			
Finances			
Fun			

Figure 6. Belief Assessment.

A common structural conflict appears in this key of *Know the Language*. It rears its ugly head when answering the question, "What does that mean I believe about myself in this dimension?" Almost without fail, our current creations (life right now) are not a reflection of what we are truly capable of creating. Peak performance is blocked by the fact that most people suffer from low self-esteem, a poor self-image or a lack of self-confidence. Jack Canfield, in his compact disc set *Maximum Confidence: Ten Secrets of Extreme Self-Esteem*, states two out of three people suffer from low self-esteem. If you don't have confidence in your abilities, you won't take the creative risks necessary to build the vision for the great life you so richly deserve. If low self-esteem is a structural conflict for you, it is limiting your ability to live your greatness. To help offset this conflict, we encourage you to listen to *Maximum Confidence: Ten Secrets of Extreme Self-Esteem*. It will transform you!

In the compact disc set *The New Psycho-Cybernetics: A Mind Technology for Living Your Life Without Limits*, Dr. Maxwell Maltz and Dan Kennedy spend time unraveling the limits of the self-image. The basic premise of Psycho-Cybernetics is that one cannot achieve beyond the self-image held in the mind. Maltz and Kennedy offer many methods and strategies for reprogramming the self-image. This compact disc set is another transforming program that we highly recommend to you to further combat the structural conflicts of low self-esteem, poor self-image or a lack of self-confidence.

Repeating situations can also reveal patterns of behavior that need to be changed. For instance, have you ever had the feeling that the same thing keeps happening to you over and over. In other words, it is the moment when you say to yourself, "Why does this keep happening to me?" Well, it keeps happening to you because you keep creating the same situation by repeating the same choices. To change the pattern, different choices are required. Only then have you raised your awareness to exercise your power to break the pattern. In order to become more aware of repeating patterns, perform an analysis of each of the dimensions of The Great Life System using the Repeating Patterns Assessment tool in Figure 7. Think of situations that repeatedly happen to you in each dimension. As part of the assessment, ask yourself these three questions about that repeating pattern, answering in the space provided in Figure 7:

1. "What does the mirror show me about a behavior pattern I keep repeating?"

2. "What is the lesson in this behavior pattern that I am missing?"

3. "The next time this situation occurs, what better choice can I make?"

Dimension	What does the mirror show me about a behavior pattern I keep repeating?	What is the lesson in this behavior pattern that I am missing?	The next time this situation occurs, what better choice can I make?
Self			
Family			
Faith			
Friends			
Finances			
Fun			

Figure 7. Repeating Patterns Assessment.

This assessment is another great place to employ the AWE method: Analyze, Write, and Explain. From this information you should be able to discern why you keep engaging in a disadvantageous repeating behavior pattern. That knowledge empowers you to choose differently next time the same situation occurs.

Many times when people are engaging in self-analysis, the ego does the *I don't know* dance to protect itself. Because the ego wants to protect itself at all cost, it can't allow the rest of your mind to discover the truth. Thus, anytime a question threatens the way the ego functions, the ego whispers the answer *I don't know* inside your head so you answer that way. Usually, when you say you don't know why something is the way it is, the mind will stop searching for the answer. But if we want to have the great life, we can't stop searching for the answer. For this reason, we need a counter-measure to the *I don't know* dance. Each time you answer, "*I don't know*" to one of the questions in this Chapter, ask yourself this follow-up question: "But if I did know the answer, what would it be?" Don't let yourself off the hook. Ask this counter-measure question over and over until you provide an answer.

The final part of the language of The Great Life System is entrenched in the concept that we are limitless. What is difficult for most of us to comprehend and accept is that the only limits on our personal universe are the ones we place on ourselves. We limit ourselves in the way that we think, in the way that we talk, and in the way that we fail to dream big. We need to stop using limiting language. We need to believe the world is our playground. We need to believe we deserve it all. We need to create Big Hairy Audacious Goals (BHAGs) and then believe we can meet those goals. Go big or go home!

One of the more profound books on removing self-imposed limitations is Victoria Castle's (2007) *Trance of Scarcity*. She talks about the limiting stories we tell ourselves, because at one point those stories served a purpose for us and now they have become part of who we are (and we keep the stories even if they no longer serve us). Such stories include comments like, "We never have enough," "We can never make ends meet," "I can't do anything right," "Life is hard," "There is never enough time," "I could never afford that," or "What could possibly happen next?" Her book shares with the reader ways to acknowledge the old story, let it go, and write a new, more empowering story.

To help overcome our self-imposed limits, we need to look at our own stories. The best way to examine our own stories is to complete the Storytelling Assessment in Figure 8. Examine each of the dimensions of The Great Life System by asking yourself the four questions below and recording you answers in the space provided in Figure 8:

1. "What have I been telling myself about this dimension?"

2. "Is it true?"

3. "What about this story needs to change?"

4. "How can I re-write this story?"

Dimension	What have I been telling myself about this dimension?	Is it true?	What about this story needs to change?	How can I re-write this story?
Self				
Family				
Faith				
Friends				
Finances				
Fun				

Figure 8. Storytelling Assessment.

Tomi's example of how she re-wrote one of her stories will help in understanding how to begin the process of removing self-imposed limitations. Tomi had some self-limiting beliefs about money that she unknowingly adopted from her parents: (a) "There is never enough money;" (b) "I made this dollar so I can make another one;" and (c) "Another day, another dollar." Without realizing it, these stories worked in concert to limit Tomi's beliefs about financial wealth. Some mornings, upon arrival at work, she would repeat out loud at the office, "Another day, another dollar." The thoughts and values that were part of this story include Tomi's underlying beliefs that she wasn't worth more than a dollar, her work wasn't worth more than a dollar, and that she wouldn't be paid much for her work. With these negative vibrations being projected into the Divine Matrix, no wonder her financial wealth was meager.

Tomi started to shift her thinking after reading about the abundance of the universe in a metaphor about the ocean. It doesn't matter whether you show up at the ocean with a thimble, a teaspoon, a coffee mug, or a tanker truck. Whatever you bring will be filled with ease. Tomi realized that she had been showing up with a thimble, because that is all she thought she deserved. She quickly decided to get a commercial truck license and show up at work with a tanker truck each day. And why not? The only thing telling her she couldn't was her own thoughts. What thoughts keep you from driving a tanker truck to work?

After realizing her thoughts limited her beliefs about abundance, Tomi went in search of other ways to expand her thinking about abundance. She came across T. Harv Ecker's (2005) *Secrets of the Millionaire Mind*. He offers great positive self-talk that helped Tomi re-write her story. Several of the lines from her personal mantra have their roots in Ecker's book.

Another story Jerry and Tomi created about their lives was the WFC. The WFC is the White Family Curse. We cannot begin to tell you all of the crazy things that have happened to our family. To do that, this book would have to become a novel! But, at one point, the weird and wacky things that happened to Tom, Janie, and their four children became so extraordinary that Tomi began to say in those moments, "The White Family Curse strikes again!" Everyone in the family laughed when she said it, and we all started to believe in its existence. And, then more things began to happen. Everyone in the family began to believe that nothing could go right and then nothing did go right. Tomi realized she was perpetuating the strange happenings by expecting them to happen. So without announcing it, Tomi put the curse to rest by banishing WFC from her vocabulary and thoughts. Instead, she reminds herself to "expect great things today." With the WFC out of the way, the strange happenings are on the decline.

Another way to overcome our own limiting behavior is to find someone who lives a great life just like you want and emulate them. Many of us don't have a reference point or, without realizing it, default to emulating our parents or caregivers. We do so because that is what we know and feel comfortable with. If your parents are Barack and Michelle Obama or Bill and Melinda Gates, emulating your parents is a great idea! However, most of us don't have parents like that. If we want to be more and do more, we need reference points that stretch us. For instance, Tomi's reference points are John Maxwell and Robin Sharma. These remarkable men (voted the number 1 and number 2 leadership gurus in the world, respectively) have dedicated their lives to contributing to the success of others. Their impact has been globally profound. They certainly give Tomi something to stretch for in each of her dimensions.

Tomi's teenage son, Warren, wants to be a great tennis player. As part of her quest to help Warren achieve this vision, Tomi looks for stories of tennis players who have behaved in ways that make them appear limitless so she can share those with Warren. The idea is for Warren to pick one of these seemingly *limitless* tennis players as a reference point. The 2009 Australian Open provided such an opportunity. In the quarterfinals on the women's side of the Open, Serena Williams was playing Svetlana Kuznetsova. Kuznetsova was up on Williams by one set and was leading in the second set five games to three. To make the moment even more dramatic, Kuznetsova was serving and was up several match points. All Kuznetsova had to do was score one point to win game six and she would move on to the quarterfinals. Then, the magic happened. Williams dug deep into her reservoir of beliefs and fought back, winning the second set 7-5 and taking the third set handily 6-1. That match, in Tomi's mind, is one of the most remarkable shows of presence, bigness, and limitlessness by an athlete. Williams played like she had no limits, like she could do anything. Tomi uses this example with her son, Warren, to emphasize that as an athlete, the score never matters until the match is over, the horn sounds, or the referee blows the whistle. Regardless of the score, even match point when you are down a set, you are limitless and have the ability to play big and win!

Reference points allow us to see and believe that we can live bigger than where we are right now. Find out who your reference points are by asking yourself this question about each of the six dimensions: "Who is my guiding star that acts as my reference point in this dimension?" Like Tomi, you can have more than one reference point or have different reference points for different dimensions of The Great Life System. As you think about people who might qualify to be your reference point, remember they need to stretch you. You can have more than one reference point. But, above all, pick someone who has the great life you would like to have. Then start imitating their behaviors, choices, and decisions.

Tomi recently saw a phenomenal example of working to change the reference point in a December 14, 2008, segment of CBS's *60 Minutes*. The segment was on Pete Carroll, the University of California's (USC) football coach, and his efforts to reduce gang violence in Los Angeles (L.A.). The segment showed Carroll in an L.A. project late at night with a group of young African American men. The discussion among Carroll and the men focused on what the future holds for these fellows. The men answered that they saw themselves either in a gang or in a coffin. Unfortunately, death and gangs are all these men know. Carroll was offering these men a different vision of the future. He gave these guys his personal cell phone number and told them to call him. He took some of them to a USC football practice. He also challenged them to reduce the violence. Carroll's efforts to change the reference point for these men are working. Part of the segment included an interview with an L.A.P.D. gang task force member. The officer said that Carroll's efforts had given him hope and that there had been a reduction in gang violence in the area. The point of sharing this story is that changing a person's reference point does impact the vision that person will hold.

As you knock down your own barriers keep this thought in mind: Have a healthy disrespect for the impossible.

In summary, to speak the language of The Great Life System and to influence the system to your advantage, the following actions are required:

1. Treat all people and all things with respect, because we are all connected.

2. Manage your vibration and what you attract into your life by having a positive attitude and by engaging in positive self-talk.

3. Feel your future successes by acting as if they have already occurred.

4. Use the mirror to see what you created and what patterns need changing.

5. Remove self-imposed limits by changing your story and finding new reference points.

The actions listed above move you toward your great life and expand your universe outward to allow you the space to receive the abundance that will be heaped upon you. While these actions are those that you actively want to engage in to move toward the great life, there are forces at work that seek to anchor you where you are. These forces are called structural conflicts.

Fritz (1989) described structural conflict as the system involving both the tension pulling us toward our goal and the tension anchoring us to our underlying beliefs. It can also be called living in the paradox. It is a structure of conflicting forces: pulling us simultaneously toward and away from what we want. Awareness of these structural conflicts will enhance our ability to manage them when they occur. Braden (2007) indentifies the structural conflicts within the Divine Matrix as the negative thoughts we put into the universe. He states that this negativity is rooted in one of three universal fears: abandonment, low self-worth, or lack of trust.

Sandra Anne Taylor (2007), in *Quantum Success*, explains the effect of such negative thoughts:

> Motivations that are founded in fear or filled with doubt can only create a dark energy around your desire. Such emotions originate in neediness, sending out waves of repulsive energy. Fear's negative signal is clear, and the message is: I'm incapable. I'm undeserving. I'm lost…
>
> The emotions of fear and doubt eclipse all of the positive-energy boosters that you could project… (p. 20)

Fear is primarily based in rejection and failure. No one wants to be rejected and no one wants to fail. Thus, our grandest hopes and biggest goals generate mixed emotions in us, because we want to succeed, but we don't want to fail or be rejected along the way. As Taylor (2007) further explains:

On the one hand, you may tell yourself that you want to be successful—that's the first driving intention. On the other hand, a defeating experience or a limiting belief may lead you to believe that it isn't possible—and that also becomes an energetic intention.

...your desires are both desperate and *dis*parate (or opposite), and these intentions fight each other in the energetic realm. (p. 21)

Ecker (2005) discusses this same structural conflict. When he began to examine his beliefs, he recognized that

Even though I said I really wanted to be rich, I had some deep-rooted worries about it. Mostly I was afraid. Afraid that I might fail, or worse, succeed and then somehow lose it all. Then I'd really be a schmuck. Worse, I could blow the one thing I had going for me: my "story" that I had all this "potential." (pp. 3-4)

Certain feelings act as a repulsive vibration that pushes away what you seek. These feelings include desperation and urgency. Also, forcing a situation or trying to push to make things happen repels rather than attracts what you want. To counter desperation, urgency and force, we must learn to let go of outcomes and rest in the understanding that all things that happen do so for our greatest good.

In this Chapter we described our research process to find a scientifically provable theory that explains how the universe operates. We sought to find a language of the universe and we found its basis in the Divine Matrix. By using Einstein's assumption that everything is energy, and through the science of physics and the understanding of the Divine Matrix, we are able to comprehend how energy behaves and harness that knowledge to understand how our universe behaves. By using the principles of the container, the bridge, and the mirror, we understand the external methods for influencing the structure itself. We also gained understanding of how negative thoughts act as a structural conflict, limiting our ability to influence The Great Life System. In the next Chapter we continue to construct The Great Life System by examining the internal influences that shape the functioning of the system.

CHAPTER 4

Key 3: Know the Mental Models

Try not to become a man of success but rather to become a man of value.
—*Albert Einstein*

The key of *Know the Mental Models* is about those patterns, thoughts, or beliefs that shape how we act. In other words, the internal influences which determine how we function in each moment. Everyone has these Mental Models, but most of us are not aware of them or the force they exert in our lives. Mental Models manifest themselves internally in the Self as values. Mental Models manifest themselves externally from the Self to the 5Fs as actions. These actions operate as a bridge between the Self and the other dimensions. Thus, knowing our values allows us to leverage their strength to propel us ever closer to the great life. Over the course of this Chapter, we explain Mental Models, values, and how these values act as the bridge between the Self and the 5Fs. By doing this, we continue to expand upon The Great Life System by explaining these internal influences and their impact on how the Self functions within the system.

A mental model is an explanation in someone's thought process for how something works in the real world (Senge, 1994). A mental model is a kind of internal symbol or representation of external reality that plays a major role in cognition and decision-making. Once formed, Mental Models may replace carefully considered analysis as a means of conserving time and energy. Mental Models are deeply ingrained assumptions, generalizations, and internal images of how the world works, images that limit us to familiar ways of thinking and acting. Very often, we are not consciously aware of our Mental Models or the effects they have on our behavior.

As The Great Life System was designed by Jerry and Tomi, the Mental Model of values is the component of the system that must be understood and leveraged in order for change to take place. Values are the deepest beliefs and sentiments to which we subscribe. A value is a belief, a mission, or a philosophy that is meaningful. Whether we are consciously aware of them or not, every individual has a core set of personal values. Values can range from the simple, such as the belief in hard work and honesty, to the more complex, such as wisdom, unity, or inner peace (Posner, 2008). Whatever values we have, they are the driving force in our life. They are the reason we see our universe as it is and the rationale for our actions within that universe. Values are the rules by which we make decisions about right and wrong, should and shouldn't, good and bad. Posner (2008) explained values in *A New Way of Living:*

> Values drive us, motivate us, move life, move us forward -- enabling progress even evolution. Values are what enable us to take the Next Step —whether they drive our own individual lives in a positive direction; improve the economic, social, and cultural conditions of a nation; or, move society forward in its never-ending ascending path of progress. (p. 222)

Values are indispensable to The Great Life System. "The key point to keep in mind about values is that implementing them energizes everything concerned with it. For an individual committing to and applying values releases fresh energies, which always attract success, achievement, and well-being" (Posner, 2008, p. 7). If you really want to unpack your great life, then it is imperative to understand your values and their force and influence in your personal universe. In order to do so, we have to understand what values we operate by.

The proposition that people rely on Mental Models was first put forward by the Scottish psychologist Kenneth Craik. In *The Nature of Exploration*, Craik (1943) wrote that the mind constructs "small-scale models" of reality that it uses to reason, to anticipate events, and to underlie explanation. Mental Models are representations of reality that people use to understand specific phenomena. Gentner and Stevens (1983), in *Mental Models*, described them as follows: "In interacting with the environment, with others, and with the artifacts of technology, people form internal Mental Models of themselves and of the things with which they are interacting. These models provide predictive and explanatory power for understanding the interaction" (p. 7). Johnson-Laird (1983) proposed Mental Models as the basic structure of cognition: "It is now plausible to suppose that Mental Models play a central and unifying role in representing objects, states of affairs, sequences of events, the way the world is, and the social and psychological actions of daily life" (p. 397).

Mental Models are subtle but powerful (Arango, 1998). *Subtle* because we usually are unaware of their effect. *Powerful* because they determine what we pay attention to; therefore, what we do. When left unchallenged, they cause us to see what we have always seen: the same needs, the same opportunities, the same results. And, because we see what our Mental Models permit us to see, we do what our Mental Models permit us to do.

Mental Models have four main characteristics that help us understand their function:

1. Mental Models include what a person thinks is true, not necessarily what is actually true.

2. Mental Models are similar in structure to the thing or concept they represent.

3. Mental Models allow a person to predict the results of his or her actions.

4. Mental Models are simpler than the thing or concept they represent. They include only enough information to allow accurate predictions. (McDaniel, 2003, ¶3)

Values clearly reflect the key characteristics of Mental Models. First, values are what you believe to be true. They are the foundation for your views on how you want to live your life. Second, the model of values is easily understood regarding what they represent. Third, if you are living your values, it is easy to predict how you will react to situations. Finally, values are simple to understand as a mental concept and allow us to accurately predict actions. Because our values can be used to accurately predict our actions, it is fair to say we act out of habit because of our values. Without realizing it, we construct Mental Models that allow us to turn concepts into habit. These habits become the default mode for the operation of the Self in The Great Life System.

You acquire values in several ways over the course of your life. At first, values are developmental. They form as we grow, develop, and mature. Then, we unknowingly change them over time as we make certain life choices. The values that enable you to accomplish your goals are primarily drawn from your family, peers, and, secondarily, by your education. Later, our job choices supply some values and our life choices provide a few more. Values are so significant to the way we operate that we can easily point to examples that impacted the course of history.

We can trace values back to Biblical times when God delivered the Ten Commandments to Moses for the Hebrews to live by, if they wanted to enjoy a peaceful life. Here are those Commandments:

1. I am the Lord your God Who has taken you out of the land of Egypt, from the house of slavery.

2. You shall have no other gods but me.

3. You shall not take the name of your Lord in vain.

4. You shall remember and keep the Sabbath day holy.

5. Honor your father and mother.

6. You shall not kill.

7. You shall not commit adultery.

8. You shall not steal.

9. You shall not bear false witness against your neighbor.

10. You shall not covet your neighbor's goods. You shall not covet your neighbor's house. You shall not covet your neighbor's wife, nor his man-servant, nor his maidservant, nor his bull, nor his donkey, nor anything that is your neighbor's.

Another set of values that are well known are from Pope Gregory. In the 6th Century he defined the Seven Deadly Sins that should be avoided along with a counter-balancing set of values that should be followed known as the Seven Virtues. The Seven Deadly Sins, as Pope Gregory identified them, are as follows:

1. Pride is an excessive belief in one's own abilities.

2. Envy is wanting what others have, be it status, abilities, or possessions.

3. Gluttony is the desire to eat or consume more than you require.

4. Lust is a powerful craving for such as sex, power, and money.

5. Anger is the loss of rational self-control and the desire to harm others.

6. Greed is the desire for material wealth or gain.

7. Sloth is laziness and the avoidance of work.

The Seven Virtues, as Pope Gregory identified them, are as follows:

1. Faith is belief in the right things (including the virtues!).

2. Hope is taking a positive future view, that good will prevail.

3. Charity is concern for, and active helping of, others.

4. Fortitude is never giving up.

5. Justice is being fair and equitable with others.

6. Prudence is care of and moderation with money.

7. Temperance is moderation of needed things and abstinence from things which are not needed.

Another famous set of values originated with Benjamin Franklin. Franklin had a set of 13 values that he sought to live by. In his efforts to live consistent with these values, he created a discipline for himself. As we mentioned before, Senge (1994) called certain practice areas disciplines because they are activities that we must integrate into our lives—we must be disciplined about living the principles that make up each one. Franklin did just that and the practice of his discipline of a values-based life provided him a great one.

Franklin (1964) made a book in which he dedicated a page to each of the values he wanted to internalize. Using this book, Franklin examined his behavior each day and made a mark if he found he did not respect that value. His discipline included focusing on only one value each week. He said at the end of each day, he would mark the faults of the day regarding that one value. He called this daily review a plan for self-examination. Franklin observed of himself that "I was surpriz'd to find myself so much fuller of Faults than I had imagined, but I had the Satisfaction of seeing them diminish" (p. 155). The values Franklin strived to align his behavior with encompassed the following:

1. Temperance. Eat not to Dulness. Drink not to Elevation.

2. Silence. Speak not but what may benefit others or yourself. Avoid trifling Conversation.

3. Order. Let all your Things have their Places. Let each Part of your Business have its Time.

4. Resolution. Resolve to perform what you ought. Perform without fail what you resolve.

5. Frugality. Make no Expense but to do good to others or yourself: i.e. Waste nothing.

6. Industry. Lose no Time. Be always employ'd in something useful. Cut off all unnecessary Actions.

7. Sincerity. Use no hurtful Deceit. Think innocently and justly; and, if you speak, speak accordingly.

8. Justice. Wrong none, by doing Injuries or omitting the Benefits that are

your Duty.

9. Moderation. Avoid Extreams. Forbear resenting Injuries so much as you think they deserve.

10. Cleanliness. Tolerate no Uncleanness in Body, Cloaths or Habitation.

11. Tranquility. Be not disturbed at Trifles, or at Accidents common or unavoidable.

12. Chastity. Rarely use Venery but for Health or Offspring; Never to Dullness, Weakness, or the Injury of your own or another's Peace or Reputation.

13. Humility. Imitate Jesus and Socrates. (pp.149-150)

Franklin may very well have been one of the first leaders to write about reference points. In his thirteenth value, Franklin wrote "Imitate Jesus and Socrates." Many of us operate without reference points (people who live the way we would like to). Reference points provide us a visualization of where we would like to go and offer a role-model for our behavior.

The understanding of the key *Know the Mental Models* leads to the core understanding of how you (the Self) operate in The Great Life System. This understanding helps us to operate more efficiently and more effectively within the system. When you understand your values, you understand why you do what you do and work toward the goals you have in your life. When you set a vision for yourself (where you would like to be at some future point), you must have supporting values to make that vision a realization. What we know about the Mental Model of values is that it is the driving force of current behavior for the Self within The Great Life System. It can also be the force that pushes us where we want to go. Finally, values act as the bridge between the Self and the other five dimensions.

When values are implemented or are newly developed, then outer circumstances can change 10 times faster (and better) than merely trying to change things on the surface (Posner, 2008). In any plan you implement to improve your life, you must have the necessary values to achieve that plan. Every story of success is based on the implementation of your values. Just study Franklin's life. It clearly worked for him.

Everyone has a value system. Values are the foundation of why you do what you do. Decisions should be made consistent with your value system. When there is alignment between your actions and your highest priorities, there is no inner conflict. When there is misalignment between your actions and your highest priorities, inner conflict is created. Misalignment is a hindrance to the great life. Moreover, if the way you are functioning in the 5Fs is not aligned with your value system, outer conflict is created. Again, this misalignment is a hindrance to the great life. Robin Sharma (2008) called this misalignment the integrity gap. He noted "The greater the chasm between your daily commitments and your deepest values, the less your life will work (and the less happiness you will feel)" (p. 64).

Given the significant role values play in influencing and leveraging The Great Life System, it is important to know what your values are. There can be many origins for your values: religion, culture, family, friends, organizations, and society. The simplest way to discover your values is to take an inventory, ranking your values from highest to lowest to identify the top five that are your highest priorities and driving forces. This inventory can be completed by looking at a list of known values and ranking them. A set of The Great Life Value Cards has been provided for you in the Appendix. To use the cards, cut them out, spread them on a table, start reviewing and eliminating values until your top five values remain. Each card has the name of the value and a definition of the value, making it easier to understand, determine, and rank your values. If you prefer a traditional deck of cards, then you can order a deck of The Great Life Value Cards online at www.5greatkeys.com. The list of values identified in the Appendix is not all inclusive. If there is a value that is important to you and it is not included in The Great Life Value Cards, then please add it.

Once you have identified your top five values, use the Values Assessment tool in Figure 9 to determine if you have an integrity gap. To use the tool in Figure 9, first replace the headers in the first row of columns two through six (Value 1 through Value 5) with each of your top five values. Then, examine the value and the dimension and analyze your behavior by asking yourself this question: "Is my current situation/behavior in this dimension consistent with my value of X?" If the answer is yes, place a check in that cell on the assessment, and if the answer is no, leave the cell blank.

Dimension/Value	Value 1	Value 2	Value 3	Value 4	Value 5
Self					
Family					
Faith					
Friends					
Finances					
Fun					

Figure 9. Values Assessment.

When you are finished with this assessment, your Values Assessment should look similar to the one in Figure 10, which Tomi completed using her values.

Dimension/Value	Wisdom	Integrity	Family	Freedom	Fun
Self	✓	✓	✓	✓	✓
Family	✓	✓	✓	✓	✓
Faith	✓	✓	✓	✓	✓
Friends	✓	✓	✓	✓	✓
Finances		✓	✓	✓	✓
Fun	✓	✓	✓	✓	✓

Figure 10. Tomi's Values Assessment Card.

As you can see from Tomi's card, there is an integrity gap for her in the Finances dimension with her value of wisdom. This gap results from the fact that within Tomi's top values, there is a further stratification of the importance of those five values. Because Tomi values fun more than wisdom, she is driven more in the Finance dimension by fun than by wisdom. The effect of this gap is that Tomi makes decisions in the Finance dimension with fun as the highest priority. That means she does not make the wisest decisions with regard to her finances, but she has a ton of fun in the process.

Tomi does not necessarily need to change her values. Instead, awareness of what drives her behavior allows her to pause before taking action and ask herself this question: "Is the action I am about to take the best choice I can make in the moment, and is it consistent with my values?" If the answer is no, then Tomi doesn't do it. Well, sometimes she does it anyway, and then she has to clean up the fall out, but that is what we humans do. Some lessons we repeat many times before we actually learn them. But, at least Tomi makes a conscious decision to step outside her values and fully recognizes the implications of that behavior. Most of the time people are unconsciously acting outside their values and don't understand the implications of that behavior.

Franklin, in living a life of self-examination, tried to assess his integrity gap every day. As Franklin observed about himself, he never arrived at the perfection he sought but he was a much better and happier man for having tried. Franklin was considered the most remarkable of all of the founding fathers, which is impressive given the extraordinary crowd of which he was a part. It is obvious leading a values-based life made Franklin an inspiring and notable fellow and set him on the path for the great life. For this reason we recommend that a daily or weekly review of your integrity gap is optimal. That way the actions you took during that day or the previous week are still fresh in your mind when you are trying to assess whether your actions in each dimension were consistent with your top five values. This on-going review of your actions in contrast to the values that you hold raises your awareness of the choices that are guiding your life. In Chapter 7 a methodology for regularly assessing your integrity gap is provided.

Make living by your values a discipline. Discipline (or habit or routine for those of us who shy away from the charge the word discipline invokes) is important. Robin Sharma (2006) summed up its meaning:

> The golden thread of a highly successful and meaningful life is self-discipline. Discipline allows you to do all those things you know in your heart you should do but never feel like doing. Without self-discipline, you will not set clear goals, manage your time effectively, treat people well, persist through the tough times, care for your health, or think positive thoughts.

> I call the habit of self-discipline "Tough Love" because getting tough with yourself is actually a very loving gesture. By being stricter with yourself, you will begin to live life more deliberately, on your own terms rather than simply reacting to life the way a leaf floating in a stream drifts according to the flow of the current on a particular day. (p. 8)

Living consistent with your values allows you to avoid the value clash. Value clashes create different types of conflict. First, acting outside your own values can create internal conflict. Second, spending time with family and friends who don't share the same or similar values can create interpersonal conflict. Third, a place of employment can have different values, creating additional internal conflict. If you value truth and honesty, you will have a difficult time with people who do not. If you value teamwork, family, or friendship, you will more than likely put the interests of others above your own personal interests. The values you embrace and act on will determine the level of the quality of your life. Knowing what your values are brings a level of understanding and awareness about the life you are leading and the choices you are making.

Choosing to act outside your values can have severe repercussions throughout your personal universe. In order to gain a deeper understanding of people and their values, Tomi collects stories of people who *live in alignment* and of people who *live out of alignment* with their values. People's real life examples enable us to see and feel the authentic and factual impact of living or not living our values. While we dislike singling out any one person for being human, because we are all human and, therefore, imperfect, the public airing of Senator John Edwards' infidelity offers a prime example of the effects of acting without answering this question first: "Is the action I am about to take the best choice I can make in the moment, and is it consistent with my values?" If Senator Edwards had asked this question of himself before acting on his desires, he may have never stepped outside his values to sleep with Rielle Hunter. But, he didn't ask that question, and the reverberations of his choice were far reaching. He lost the public confidence. He most likely cost himself a prominent role in the Obama Administration. Questions still linger about whether Senator Edwards is the father of his ex-mistress' child, casting an ongoing cloud of distrust around him. He certainly upended his personal life and almost cost him the love of his life, his wife Elizabeth.

Selections from Bob Woodruff's interview with the Senator help us understand where he went wrong:

> WOODRUFF: Your wife, Elizabeth, is probably the most admired and beloved person in this country, she's had enormous sympathy because she's also gone through cancer, how could you have done this?

> EDWARDS: Here's what, can I explain to you what happened? First of all it happened during a period after she was in remission from cancer, that's no excuse in any possible way for what happened. This is what happened. It's what happened with me and I think happens unfortunately more often sometimes with other people… Ego. Self-focus, self-importance. Now, I was slapped down to the ground when my son Wade died in 1996, in April of 1996. But then after that I ran for the senate and I got elected to the Senate and here we go again, it's the same old thing again. Adulation, respect, admiration. Then I went from being a senator, a young senator to being considered for vice president, running for president, being a vice presidential candidate and becoming a national public figure. All of which fed a self-focus, an egotism, a narcissism that leads you to believe that you can do whatever you want. You're invincible. And there will be no consequences. And nothing, nothing could be further from the truth.

> WOODRUFF: So your assumption was that you'd just never be caught?

> EDWARDS: It was a huge judgment, mistake in judgment. But yeah, I didn't think anyone would ever know about it. I didn't. And the important thing is, how could I ever get to the place, to that place and allow myself to let that happen? (*See* http://abcnews.go.com/Blotter/story?id=5441195&page=1 for the full transcript)

We can offer some suggestions to the Senator on how he ever got to that place. He forgot to keep his values front and center. He forgot to emulate Franklin and regularly rate himself on the *Values Assessment*. He forgot to create a discipline out of living his values.

There is a fabulous scene in the movie *Moonstruck* that highlights the meaning of staying true to your values. The character played by Olympia Dukakis suspects her husband is cheating on her. She goes out for dinner by herself and meets an interesting dinner companion in a character played by John Mahoney. After dinner the man walks Olympia to her house. He wants to come in but Olympia won't let him. When he asks why, she says with great knowing, "Because I am married, and I know who I am." She then goes in the house by herself. Senator Edwards lost track of who he was. While Senator Edwards offers an extreme case of what happens when we act inconsistent with our values, and he surely had much farther to fall than many of us, it does remind us of the importance of being disciplined about living our values.

One of Tomi's favorite *living in alignment* stories is of Olympic Athlete Shawn Crawford. In the 2008 Beijing Summer Olympics, Shawn Crawford competed in the 200-meter track and field event, winning the silver medal. As you may recall, the 200-meter race was mired in controversy because Crawford's USA teammate Wallace Spearmon and the Netherlands Antilles' Churandy Martina were both disqualified for running outside their lane. Because of these disqualifications, Crawford finished second instead of fourth. As the second place finisher, Crawford was awarded the silver medal. Shortly after the Olympics, in an unprecedented show of sportsmanship, Crawford gave the silver medal to Martina. According to Crawford, Martina infringed upon no other runner and he deserved the silver medal. In that moment, Crawford represented everything that sports should be about. He was living in alignment with his value that the athlete who trains and wins deserves the honor of victory.

In *Fierce Conversations*, Susan Scott (2004) offers a more detailed example of living in and out of alignment:

> Integrity requires alignment of our values—the core beliefs and behaviors that we have claimed as important to us—and our actions. So if, for example, you say that you value time with your family members yet haven't spent much time with them lately, you are, by your own definition, out of integrity. If you have taken the stand that fidelity in marriage is essential, and you're cheating on your spouse, you're out of integrity. If you tell yourself that honesty is important, yet you frequently bend the truth in an attempt to stay out of trouble or get what you want, you are out of integrity. (p. 53)

Jerry and Tomi developed a strategy for living aligned with your values. Each time you take action, you want that action to be consistent with your values so that you are living in integrity. So before taking action, ask yourself, "Is this going to move me forward?" If the answer is no, then this action is not in alignment with your values, and you should stop, drop, and roll. Stop and laugh; drop that action and roll on to something new that is aligned with your values. By choosing to live consistent with your values, you are living intentionally and are on the way to your great life.

Another benefit of understanding the Mental Model of values is knowing what your family and friends value. This knowledge brings a new level of understanding and awareness to you about the life they are leading and the choices they are making. Tomi has an example of this. She learned what her values are by participating in a values activity in a leadership class. She decided to have her family participate in the same activity. What a profound moment that was. Using a deck of values cards, Tomi had her husband, Jim, and her two sons, Shep and Warren, pick their top five values. Tomi also picked hers. Each person shared their top five values and why each value was important. Tomi, Jim, Shep, and Warren had several similar values but it was Shep's revelation of his value of independence that offered Tomi an *ah-ha* moment. No one else in the family placed independence in their top five values. This information changed Tomi's approach to Shep's behavior on some issues. For the last few years, Shep had been more and more reluctant to participate in family activities. It was frustrating for Tomi. She also noticed Warren's frustration with Shep's actions. Tomi and Warren internalized Shep's behavior as a rejection of them and what they were doing. But during the values discussion that stance shifted. When Shep identified independence as a top five value, Tomi immediately realized that Shep's reluctance to participate in family activities wasn't a rejection of her or Warren but a need to align his actions with his values. Once Tomi understood this, she was able to better address her own feelings and Warren's. Instead of seeing Shep's actions as a rejection of spending time with them, Tomi and Warren see it as Shep's need for independence (which is all it is). Tomi and Warren's feelings have been hurt a lot less, because they understand why Shep does what he does. Thus, the advantage to understanding not only what motivates you but what motivates those around you is huge.

Using the tools in this Chapter may lead you to determine that your values and your actions are not aligned, resulting in conflict. If you are unhappy with the quality of your life and the level of conflict in it, a value change may be in order. As your values change, so will your attitudes and behaviors. This can be healthy or unhealthy, positive or negative. If you decide that your values are not consistent with the great life you desire, a value shift is in order. As you make a shift, spend time on defining those values that will take you where you want to go. Make positive, healthy value changes. A new reference point that practices the values you want to incorporate into your life is a good place to start.

In this Chapter the discussion focused on values and their influence on our daily activities. Through an increased understanding of the Key of *Know the Mental Models*, we can work to align the Self with the 5Fs by taking actions that are consistent with our values. With the close of this Chapter, you have the complete structure of The Great Life System (the *know*): the system, the language of the system (external operation), and the language of the Self (internal operation). The remainder of the book is devoted to explaining application of the system (the *how*).

CHAPTER 5

Key 4: How to Use the Looking Glass

If you don't know where you are going, any road will do.
—Lewis Carroll

We were raised to be problem-solvers. The underlying structure of being a problem-solver means we sit around waiting for a problem to develop so we can solve it. We are passive until a dilemma is presented to us. Sometimes, we like the excitement of problem solving so much we actively create problems just so we can solve them. We love drama, because deep within the drama is a problem to be solved! But, this fundamental life stance of waiting on problems to arrive, creating problems, or looking for drama, doesn't help us create the great life we desire. That's because we are sitting on our hands waiting for something, anything, to show up that we can solve. If we want to create the great life, we can't be passive, we must be proactive. We can't sit back and wait. We must stop creating drama and start creating the great life instead. We must stand up, step up, and show up in our great life. The primary way to do that is to design the life you want through intentional creation.

Intentional creation is about consciously choosing what we want in this life and then relentlessly marching toward that vision with compassion and kindness. There are three steps to creating what you want:

1. Identify what you want to create;

2. Understand what currently exists; and,

3. Take action. (Fritz, 1989)

In this Chapter we use the looking glass (the mirror of the Divine Matrix) to see what we want to intentionally create (vision), and what we have unintentionally created (current reality). Taking these actions begins the process of understanding how to maximize function of the Self within the system. What we want to create is the vision we hold for ourselves. It is a future state and reflects the purpose of your life. Seeing where we are is our current reality. It is the state of all six dimensions in this moment, but not with the sugar coating and the rose colored classes. It is seeing the naked, unadulterated truth of every aspect of our lives in this moment. Susan Scott (2004) calls this *bone crushing reality.*

Mike Vance, co-author of *Think Out of the Box* (1995), worked as the Dean of Disney University. He spent a lot of time with Walt Disney. Through his work with Disney, Vance realized vision is a critical element in the blueprint for success. Disney understood that what you want to create should set your soul on fire, lighting a passion within you that keeps you marching toward the vision no matter what is taking place around you. Vance tells a remarkable story about Disney's belief in his vision. As Disney lay in a Burbank hospital dying, a reporter persistently tried to see Disney even though the hospital staff was not obliging:

> When he finally managed to get into the room, Walt couldn't sit up in bed or talk above a whisper. Walt instructed the reporter to lie down on the bed, next to him, so he could whisper in the reporter's ear. For the next 30 minutes, Walt and the journalist lay side by side as Walt referred to an imaginary map of Walt Disney World on the ceiling above the bed.

> Walt pointed out where he planned to place various attractions and buildings. He talked about transportation, hotels, restaurants, and many other parts of his vision for a property that wouldn't be open to the public for another six years.

> We told this reporter's moving experience, relayed through a nurse, to each one of our organizational development (OD) groups… the story of how a man who lay dying in the hospital whispered in the reporter's ear for 30 minutes describing his vision for the future and the role he would play in it for generations to come.

> That is the way to live—believing so much in your vision that even when you're dying, you whisper it into another person's ear. (1995, p. 30)

Fritz (1989) noted that "Vision has power, for through vision you can easily reach beyond the ordinary to the extraordinary. Vision can help you organize your actions, focus your values, and clearly see what is relevant in current reality" (p. 138).

To discover what you truly want to create, ask yourself this question: "What do *I* want?" The answer should be around the *result* you are looking for, not the process. To get at the *what* in this question, ask yourself more questions: "What am I passionate about?" "What do I love to do?" "What makes me happy?" Work through these questions to define what it is you want to create. Feel free to make up anything and set no boundaries for yourself. If no one laughed at your dreams this week, then you aren't dreaming big enough! Most importantly, don't worry about the process of creation, worry only about the result. We will return to this analysis later in this Chapter.

The second step is to know what currently exists in your world. A dose of bone crushing reality is required here as it is only upon truly understanding where we are, can we get where we are going. MapQuest provides an analogy of the significance of this information. In order to obtain directions from Map-Quest, you must enter a starting point and an ending point. A starting point is required because you can't get there from here if you don't know where *here* is. An ending point is required, too, because how can you get there if you don't know where *there* is? Thus, MapQuest requires these two data points so accurate directions can be provided. Life operates the same way. If you don't know your current location, you can't get accurate directions to your destination. If you don't know what your destination is, you can't get accurate directions to it from your current location. No wonder many of us seem to be wandering aimlessly—we have no idea where we are or where we are going!

The best place to start is to figure out where you are. While this step sounds easy, it is complicated. Some of us see reality better than it really is (the eternal optimist). Some of us see reality worse than it really is (the eternal pessimist). Our inability to size ourselves up creates challenges. As we go about the work of our great life, it is important to be candid about where we are. Fortunately, the good news is that you have already started the candid assessment of your current reality by completing The Great Life Profile. Later in this Chapter we will examine this Profile more closely. But, before we move to that, there is more to learn about the relationship between vision and current reality.

Many times we feel so overwhelmed by where we are that we can't think about where we want to go. Fritz (1989) offers an ideal summation of this feeling:

> As you begin to consider what you want to create in your life, it is good for you to know that the circumstances that presently exist are not the determining factor of the results you desire to create. You are not limited by them, even though it may seem you are entrenched in them. (p. 48)

Your past does not dictate your future. You are a limitless being who needs to provide some direction to the mind. By staking out where we are and where we want to go, we create a discrepancy or a gap. Fritz calls this gap *structural tension*. What we know about tension is that it seeks to resolve itself. Fritz uses a rubber band example to clarify the meaning of this tension. When a rubber band is pulled taut, there is a tension between the ends that seeks to bring one of the ends of the rubber band toward the other. Structural tension works the same way. When there is a discrepancy between where you are and where you want to go, that tension seeks to resolve itself. It does so by either moving toward completion of the vision or moving back to the current reality. The beauty here is that the structural tension caused by the gap is the energy we can use to drive us toward our vision. Unfortunately, systems don't like tension so the system itself will seek to return to current reality. Thus, the natural tendency is to remain in the current reality.

The tension we reference has driven many people to greatness; to achievements others thought not possible. We see this so often in sports. Michael Phelps' eight gold medals in the 2008 Beijing Summer Olympic Games come to mind. Not many people believed Phelps could accomplish such a feat. Even other swimming greats like Australia's Ian Thorpe thought it impossible. But Phelps did it. The Boston Celtics were down by 24 points to the L.A. Lakers in Game 4 of the 2008 NBA finals. Most fans had written off the Celtics in that game, but not the Celtics. They believed so much that they came back from this large deficit and won. Tiger Woods *won* the 2008 U.S. Open playing with a double stress fracture of the tibia. Woods told his doctor he was going to play injured, and he was going to win. And he did just that. When people have a vision they passionately believe in, amazing and magical things happen. There are no limits to what can be achieved. So don't limit your vision, because you think the vision is not possible. When you impose such limitations, you misrepresent the truth of what you really want and extraordinary things are not as likely to happen when you do that.

Po, the Panda in the *Dreamworks* movie *Kung Fu Panda,* demonstrated many of the principles offered here about the structure of your life. Po worked in his father's noodle shop. Po's father is Mr. Ping, a goose. Mr. Ping uses a family recipe in the restaurant that has a secret ingredient. Mr. Ping wants Po to spend his life working in the noodle shop, but Po wants to be a Kung Fu master. Given Po's size, lack of agility, and Mr. Ping's constant demands on Po to run the family noodle shop, realization of this dream seems unlikely. Yet, Po is willing to stand in the messiness of his life that is derived from the creative tension between where he is (working in the Noodle Shop) and where he wants to be (a Kung Fu Master).

One day, word spreads through town that Master Oogway (similar to the town elder) is going to select the next Dragon Warrior to fight an evil nemesis, Tai Lung, who is planning to return to town to claim his alleged rightful place as the Dragon Warrior. All of the villagers gather to watch the selection process for the next Dragon Warrior. Po is desperate to watch, too, but Mr. Ping wants

Po to take the noodle cart and sell noodles at the event. As expected (because there would be no movie unless it happened), Po is selected to be the Dragon Warrior. Po's new trainer, Master Shifu, does everything in his power to make Po quit. The other warriors also want to see Po quit, because he does not fit the image of a Dragon Warrior. Master Shifu and the other warriors cannot believe Po is the Dragon Warrior. He is out of shape and undisciplined. Po realizes he achieved his dream in name only and wants to quit. This juncture is a critical one in the creative process and what Po chooses to do next is vital to his success.

Many of us often find ourselves in the same place as Po when trying to realize our dreams. There are people who want to pull us back to the status quo (current reality) for whatever reason or they nix our dreams. Mr. Ping wanted Po to help him run the Noodle Shop not be a Kung Fu master. Master Shifu and the other warriors didn't believe Po had what it takes to be the Dragon Warrior. Po even doubted himself. These types of tension pull us back toward current reality, and in some instances, cause us to let go of our vision. Po realizes he must convince himself, his master, and the other warriors he is the real Dragon Warrior. Po is again standing in the messiness of his life that is derived from the creative tension between where he is (working in the Noodle Shop) and where he wants to be (a Kung Fu Master).

Po ultimately earns the respect of Master Shifu and the other warriors. Apparently, when it comes to getting food, Po is extremely agile. Master Shifu sees how to leverage these food-getting skills into Kung Fu warrior skills. Because Po is turned into a great warrior, he is given the sacred Dragon Scroll. This Scroll is supposed to bestow great power upon whoever reads it. When Po opens it up, there is nothing on the Scroll. In fact, the texture of the Scroll is like a mirror and only shows Po his reflection. Po and Master Shifu panic when they realize Po has no extra powers bestowed upon him by reading the Scroll and is not likely to defeat Tai Lung. Master Shifu orders everyone to leave the valley before Tai Lung appears.

As Po is making his way out of town, he sees his father who wants Po to push the noodle cart to the next town. Po is no longer the Dragon Warrior but the son of a noodle maker. Again Po is faced with tension that is pulling him back toward current reality. Many of us, in our own lives, let go of our visions at this point to resolve the tension. A poignant conversation between Po and Mr. Ping at this moment in which Mr. Ping reveals the secret ingredient of the noodle soup is that there is no secret ingredient. Mr. Ping explains people become special only when they believe they are. In that moment, Po grasps what his father has just said is the same message of the Dragon Scroll: Po is responsible for creating the specialness in his life. Po gathers himself and takes action. Po and Tai Lung engage in a ferocious battle that Po wins. Once Po realized only he could make himself special, he was able to obtain his dream of being the Dragon Warrior.

In our lives, we find the same tensions exist between where we are and where we want to be. We find people who make demands on us that are not consistent with our dreams. They want to anchor us to the status quo. Standing in this creative tension can be an unsavory place to be. You may find yourself asking such questions as, "What I am doing here?" or "Why do I want this so much?" Better yet, you may hear yourself proclaiming, "I don't seem to be getting anywhere." Periods of feeling overwhelmed or desperate are common. In that moment, we have to remember we are sitting in creative tension. We have to take responsibility for creating what we want and then relentlessly march toward that with compassion and kindness. If Po had given up on his dream of being the Dragon Warrior, he would have lived out his life in the Noodle Shop looking for the secret ingredient. How many of us wilt under the creative tension and give up on our dreams? So many of us suffer from the Noodle Effect—we let go instead of persevere. But, Po didn't. He didn't let the noodles tie him down. He found his dream and then relentlessly marched toward it. And, that is what you have to do if you want the great life.

Kung Fu Panda offers one more valuable lesson about the way the world works. Once you select the *what*, the *how* will show up. Po had no idea how he would become a Kung Fu Master, but he knew he wanted to be one. Because he held on to his vision, a path was created for him by the return of Tai Lung. Once you are clear about what it is you truly want, be open to receiving how that is delivered to you. One way we limit ourselves is by being adamant about how something must show up in our lives. Don't limit the way the *how* happens. Just keep an open mind and listen and watch, because once you put the thought out there, the universe starts working on a plan.

Bob Anderson, founder and president of the Leadership Circle, offers these words of wisdom on choosing and what it feels like:

> …committing yourself before you know how you will do what you say you will do, before it feels perfectly safe, (sic) to make the commitment, and before you know with certainty that it is even possible. I use the word "choice" for this kind of commitment. To choose a result is to commit yourself to it, in spite of all the reasons why that choice may not seem feasible or risk free. Making the choice is the fundamental act; and everything follows from that…

> …Choice is a leap. It demands faith. Those who are practiced in this

discipline have also developed a faith in forces beyond our own efforts... the universe is providential. When we fully commit ourselves, larger forces are there to work with us. (Retrieved on March 3, 2009, from: http://www.theleadershipcircle.com/site/pdf/pp-leadership-uncommon-sense.pdf, p. 17)

American Idol contestant Elliot Yamin is a real-life example of once you select the *what*, the *how* will show up. Yamin finished third in season five of Fox's *American Idol*. During an interview, Yamin said that he was at work in a drug-store in Richmond, Virginia, wondering what he could do with his big voice. During the interview, the emotion in his voice, almost desperation, was haunting. He knew he was supposed to be doing something, but he didn't know how to get there. Yamin knew what he wanted, though, and he made a choice to sing. Providence then worked on a plan for him. *American Idol* came along and the rest is history.

In the Chapter on *Know the Language*, you began to look at your current reality by asking these questions:

1. What is the mirror telling me about what I have created in this dimension, and what that means I believe about myself?

2. What is the mirror telling me about a behavior pattern I keep repeating, and what is the lesson in this behavior pattern that I am missing?

3. What am I pretending not to know?

At this point, we return to the looking glass to delve more deeply into current reality. Below are the instructions for assessing the current reality of each of the six dimensions in greater detail. Have your Great Life Profile available as you work through the tools below. As you assess your current reality, one of the most important things you can do is to be accurate and truthful. Yes, we keep hammering the head of that nail but knowing exactly where you are right now is vital to where you are going. No matter how harsh you may feel the current reality is, or how unhappy you are about it, take the rose-colored glasses off and let truth flow.

Gawain (2000) offers this explanation of why it is important to understand current reality:

The dawning awareness about *what doesn't work* in how we are living is by far the most powerful step in our growth. It is also the most difficult and uncomfortable. As soon as we recognize a problem, we are on the road to healing it. However, that healing takes time. Meanwhile, we may have to watch ourselves repeat the same old self-defeating patterns a few more times. (p. 112)

Take stock of where you are, and take ownership of where you are, because you created this life, and you are responsible for it. As you take stock, recognize there are elements of caring and compassion in this process. In this moment, there is no one to blame for your current reality. Forgive yourself if you don't like where you are by understanding that you didn't know any better. Understand that you didn't know a different method, so you did what you knew. But, after reading this book, you will know better, and you will have a different method. In fact, respect yourself for what you have created to date. Shift your thinking to, "Hey, I was wise enough to create this (even if it is a mess). I can create something new and better!" Recognizing you created your entire life circumstances stirs feelings of awareness and authority within. It allows you to see who you are. It allows you to confidently and fully step into your Self. It allows you to create your future with a conscious awareness of all that you are, and that you don't require anyone else's approval or recognition to create all that you want.

Self: To assess the current reality of the Self, we recommend using the Self Current Reality Assessment in Figure 11. Gaze into a looking glass and ask yourself if you think your relationship with your Self is healthy or unhealthy. As a part of this analysis, ask if you see any of these five things in your Self:

1. Someone who places the blame on someone, or something else, or who always has an excuse.

2. Someone who runs away from problems or reacts instead of responds to problems.

3. Someone who constantly criticizes others or sits in judgment of others.

4. Someone who waits for others to rescue them.

5. Someone who pretends that everything is hunky-dory. (Harris, 2007)

We suggest using the AWE method explained in Chapter 3 to answer these questions. Record your reflections in the space provided in Figure 11. Finally, keep in mind The Great Life Profile score for Self as you complete this assessment.

Self	Yes	No	Why
Am I someone who places the blame on someone or something else or who always has an excuse?			
Am I someone who runs away from problems or reacts instead of responds to problems			
Am I someone who constantly criticizes others or sits in judgment of others?			
Am I someone who waits for others to rescue them?			
Am I someone who pretends that every-thing is hunky dory?			

Figure 11. Self Current Reality Assessment.

As you analyze your answers, use the following information as a guide. People who place blame, make excuses, or who run away from their problems are refusing to take responsibility for their lives and what they have created. Absolutely everything is a choice. You chose, whether you realized it or not, to get out of bed this morning, to show up at work today and to be there on time. You chose where to go to lunch and what to have for lunch. Your educational choices 15 years ago now impact your career choices today. Your choice to have premarital sex resulted in you having a baby out of wedlock. Your choices to eat biscuits for breakfast and eat ice cream for dessert every night for the last 5 years are the reasons why your pants don't fit today. Your choice to act as a friend to your teenager, instead of his or her parent, is why your child acts like there are no rules and why your child walks all over you. But, you get the point—everything in your life in this moment is a result of every choice you made along the way.

As you develop the Profile for the Self, be aware of the fatal flaw profile. A fatal flaw is a behavior that shatters the ability to achieve the great life. The only solution to the fatal flaw profile is to fix it. The internal fatal flaw behavior for the Self is excessiveness. A *too mucher* impedes progress by doing too many drugs, by drinking too much alcohol, by smoking too much, and by gambling too much. Over-eating and under-eating can also be fatal flaw profiles if they compromise your good health. If you have a fatal flaw profile, then please seek help immediately from a qualified professional.

Family: To assess the current reality of Family, we recommend using the Family Current Reality Assessment in Figure 12. Gaze into a looking glass and take these actions:

1. Identify the five family members you spend the most time with (include spouse or significant other) and insert their names in the first column of rows two through six in Figure 12 (replacing Family Member 1 through Family Member 5).

2. Ask yourself this question: "Does this person bring out the best in me?"

3. Ask yourself this question: "Does this person want what is best for me?"

4. Ask yourself this question: "Is this person's actions consistent with their words?"

5. For each of these questions, ask yourself this follow-up question: "What makes me believe this?"

Use the AWE method to answer these questions. Record your reflections in the space provided in Figure 12. Finally, keep in mind The Great Life Profile score for Family as you complete this assessment.

Family	Does this person bring out the best in me?	Does this person want what is best for me?	Does this person behave in a manner consistent with their verbal support?	What makes me believe this?
Family Member 1				
Family Member 2				
Family Member 3				
Family Member 4				
Family Member 5				

Figure 12. Family Current Reality Assessment.

Faith: In Chapter 5 a current assessment was completed on the Mental Model of values. Use those assessment results here as your current reality for this dimension.

Friends: To assess the current reality of Friends, we recommend using the Friends Current Reality Assessment in Figure 13. Gaze into a looking glass and ask yourself if you think your relationships with your friends are healthy or unhealthy. As part of this analysis, take these actions:

1. Identify the five friends you spend the most time with and insert their names in the first column of rows two through six in Figure 13 (replacing Friends 1 through Friends 5).

2. Ask yourself this question: "Does this person bring out the best in me?"

3. Ask yourself this question: "Does this person want what is best for me?"

4. Ask yourself this question: "Is this person's actions consistent with their words?"

5. For each of these questions, ask yourself this follow-up question: "What makes me believe this?"

Use the AWE method to answer these questions. Record your reflections in the space provided in Figure 13. Finally, keep in mind The Great Life Profile score for Friends as you complete this assessment.

Friends	Does this person bring out the best in me?	Does this person want what is best for me?	Does this person behave in a manner consistent with their verbal support?	What makes me believe this?
Friend 1				
Friend 2				
Friend 3				
Friend 4				
Friend 5				

Figure 13. Friends Current Reality Assessment.

Finances: To assess the current reality of Finances, we recommend using the Finances Current Reality Assessment in Figure 14. Gaze into a looking glass and ask yourself if you think your relationship with your finances is healthy or unhealthy. Finances mean career wealth, economic wealth, and impact wealth. Career wealth is your level of job satisfaction, including insurance like health and disability insurance, career satisfaction, and salary satisfaction. Economic wealth represents your net worth, including items like savings, income, valuables, investments, and retirement plans. Impact wealth means time or money. It is the ability to donate your time or your money to organizations of your choice, including your church.

As part of this analysis, take these actions:

1. Ask yourself this question: "Am I satisfied in the career wealth department?" (This means your level of job satisfaction, career satisfaction, and salary satisfaction.)

2. Ask yourself this question: "Am I satisfied in the economic wealth department?" (This means your net worth, including items like savings, income, valuables, investments, and retirement plans.)

3. Ask yourself this question: "Am I satisfied in the impact wealth department?" (This means time or money. It is the ability to donate your time or your money to organizations of your choice, including your church.)

4. For each of these questions, ask yourself this follow-up question: "Why?"

Use the AWE method to answer these questions. Record your reflections in the space provided in Figure 14. Finally, keep in mind The Great Life Profile score for Finances as you complete this assessment.

Finances	Yes	No	Why
Am I satisfied with my life insurance and health insurance?			
Am I satisfied with my job?			
Am I satisfied with my career?			
Am I satisfied with my salary?			
Am I satisfied with my net worth?			
Am I satisfied with the amount of money I donate to charities?			
Am I satisfied with the amount of time I donate to charities?			

Figure 14. Finances Current Reality Assessment.

Fun: To assess the current reality of Fun, we recommend using the Fun Current Reality Assessment in Figure 15. Gaze into a looking glass and ask yourself if you are having fun in your life. Fun means those activities you engage in for rest and relaxation including hobbies and interests. Examples include reading, playing on the computer, surfing the web, electronic games, bowling, hiking, boating, bike riding, swimming, watching movies, cooking, hunting, skiing, and the like. For the adults in the group, Fun also includes sex and intimacy. Finally, Fun is about the laughter in your life.

In *Think Out of the Box,* Vance (1995) describes a story he read in *USA Today* on laughter. He said, "A story featured in USA Today reported that the average child laughs about 400 times per day. The article went on to say that the average adult laughs only 15 times per day. What happened to the other 385 laughs?" (1995, p. 20). We don't know where those laughs went, but we highly recommend you spend some time each day finding them! Rent a funny video. Buy a joke book and read it. Watch a funny television show. Find funny videos on UTube (there are plenty of those!). Check out some funny cat pictures at www.icanhascheezburger.com. Seek laughter proactively. It will make your life better.

As part of your Fun analysis, take these actions:

1. Identify the five activities you do for fun and list them in the first column in rows two through six of Figure 15.

2. Ask yourself this question: "When was the last time I engaged in this activity?"

3. Ask yourself this question: "What can I do to include this activity in my life more often?"

4. Ask yourself this question: "When was the last time I laughed so hard I cried?"

5. Ask yourself this question: "What can I do to bring more laughter into my life?"

Use the AWE method to answer these questions. Record your reflections in the space provided in Figure 15. Finally, keep in mind The Great Life Profile score for Fun as you complete this assessment.

Activities	When was the last time I engaged in this activity?	What can I do to include this activity in my life more often?
Fun Activity 1		
Fun Activity 2		
Fun Activity 3		
Fun Activity 4		
Fun Activity 5		
Laughed so hard I cried		

Figure 15. Fun Current Reality Assessment.

After completing an assessment of each dimension, assimilate all that information on your Current Reality Inventory in Figure 16 by answering the big picture question of, "Is this dimension healthy and contributing to my great life?" If you believe the dimension is unhealthy, ask yourself this follow up question, "If this dimension is unhealthy, what needs to change in this dimension to be healthy?"

Dimension	Healthy/Great Life	If unhealthy, what needs to change to be healthy?
Self	❑ Yes ❑ No	
Family	❑ Yes ❑ No	
Friends	❑ Yes ❑ No	
Faith	❑ Yes ❑ No	
Finances	❑ Yes ❑ No	
Fun	❑ Yes ❑ No	

Figure 16. Current Reality Inventory.

At this point you have a clear view of your current state and understand some of what in your life might need to be transformed if you want to move in the direction of a great life. This clear view provides information you can build upon to brainstorm on the future state and determine what truly matters to you so you can create what you want. Later in this Chapter, to help clarify what you truly want, there is a Vision Assessment tool.

Because businesses have long engaged in creating visions, the business world is much farther along in understanding the significance of the vision process then we are at the individual level. Most businesses have one all encompassing vision for the whole company. Each department then develops its own vision that contributes to achievement of, and supports, the larger vision of the company (or, that is the way it should work). We are mimicking that same strategy here. Build a vision for each of the 5Fs that supports and is congruent with the vision for the Self. For example, Tomi's vision for herself is to facilitate greatness. For her, facilitating greatness manifests itself in each of the 5Fs as making people and things better. In the Family dimension, Tomi invests a lot of time in helping her children and other family members find their greatness. In the Friends dimension, Tomi invests a lot of time in helping her friends make their lives better by supporting their dreams and contributing to moving them forward however she can. For Tomi's Self, greatness means committing to personal development and growth to make herself great and to find her peak performance. Tomi has built a vision for herself and for each of the 5Fs that support what matters most to her: making life better by facilitating greatness. As you go about defining the results you want, keep in mind that you want a vision for each dimension that is consistent with the larger vision for the Self.

Discovering what you truly want is an ongoing process. Your passions and wants change throughout the course of your life. Sometimes you realize what you are marching toward isn't what you really want. You course- correct by re-defining your vision. Sometimes we achieve our vision—mission accomplished! This success also requires us to redefine our vision.

Tomi didn't have a formalized vision until she was 36. In her Ph.D. program, all students were required to find their purpose. Her vision flowed from working on finding her purpose. Since then her vision has been reframed at least once a year and sometimes twice a year. There have been times when her vision was reframed with ease. Other times, when she was standing in the creative tension, questioning her sanity, she would wonder, "What am I doing here?" Sometimes it is easy and sometimes it isn't easy. Be gentle with yourself. You are exactly where you are supposed to be.

Knowing that your vision creation is most likely in its infancy, there is a tool in Figure 17 that can be used to help develop your vision. As you use this tool, do so in collaboration with the information from the Current Reality Inventory in Figure 16. To complete the Vision Assessment, gaze into a looking glass to ask yourself these two questions:

1. What do I truly want (what lights my fire, is a passion for me)?

2. What does that look like?

Be sure to record your reflections on the Vision Assessment in Figure 17.

Dimension	What do I truly want (anything is possible)?	What does that look like?
Self		
Family		
Friends		
Faith		
Finances		
Fun		

Figure 17. Vision Assessment.

If this process for understanding where you are and where you would like to go doesn't feel right, try something else. Other methods used to discover what truly matters most to you is by writing your obituary or by writing a legacy statement. Both of these help define what you would like to leave behind and help get at what truly matters most to you.

Fritz (1989) points to a prime example of structural tension in Dr. Martin Luther King Junior's *I Have a Dream* speech. King painted two pictures in that speech. He shared the current social situation in 1963 by talking about the existing racism. But, he also painted a picture of the future state by embracing his dreams of freedom and justice. King embraced and embodied his vision. He lived it every day. And, you must do the same on the path to the great life.

If the suggestions offered here aren't successful in helping to clarify what it is you truly want, try painting the two pictures of where you are and where you would like to go by writing your own *I Have a Dream* speech. See where it takes you, and build from there!

If you want more detail and instruction on how to create what matters most in your life, Jerry and Tomi recommend two books by Robert Fritz -- *The Path of Least Resistance* and *Creating*—or Julia Cameron's *The Artist's Way*. We also recommend Myss' compact disc set, *Your Power to Create*.

As you are able to clarify what really matters most to you, and you begin to understand what you want to create, you must take *action*. You must make the key of *How to Use the Looking Glass*—to see where you are and where you are going—a discipline, routine or habit. Taking these four steps starts that process:

1. Choose your results.

2. Embody your results.

3. Receive your results.

4. Acknowledge your results. (Fritz, 1989)

Within these steps rest the structural conflicts of *How to Use the Looking Glass*. If we want the great life, it is important to be aware of and learn how to navigate these conflicts.

Part of intentionally creating your great life means owning it by choosing your results. That requires saying you *choose* what you want. Take Tomi's vision to facilitate greatness for example. She must make this statement: "I choose greatness." Jerry and Tomi's colleague, Judy Johnson, has as her vision, "Creativity is me." That means Judy must make this statement: "I choose creativity." Take action toward your vision by consciously choosing to march toward it. Announce boldly that you choose your vision. Proclaim it to the world. Don't worry what others think of you or your vision. You have to believe you are limitless and that what you truly want can be created.

You must *embody* your vision. Realign your whole life with it. Build goals and objectives around your vision that move you toward that vision every day. Goals are so important to achieving and embodying a vision. For work on goal setting, we recommend Canfield's compact disc set *Maximum Confidence: Ten Secrets of Extreme Self-Esteem*. He covers how goals should be written and their importance to achieving the results you seek. Track your progress against your goals and objectives. Live as if what you want has already happened. Once you project your thoughts into the Divine Matrix and feel as if your vision is already accomplished, the Divine Matrix mirrors that back to you.

It is imperative that we *receive* our results. So many of us don't think we are worthy of the great life so we don't have the ability to receive. Gawain (2000) provides an explanation of this phenomenon:

> Much of this viewpoint comes from our traditional transcendent religious beliefs... The less we want, the freer we are to move on to the spiritual realm. In this spiritual ideal, we strive not to need or want. This idea is so pervasive that whether or not we are religiously inclined, our model of goodness is an altruistic person who gives with no thought or desire for themselves...

> We also find it difficult to receive for psychological reasons. The giving position is essentially the power position... The receiving end of an

interaction is much more vulnerable… Our discomfort with vulnerability makes receiving very challenging for many of us. It can put us in touch with deep feelings of unworthiness. (pp. 63-64)

Often when good things happen to us we call it luck. In the past, when good things happened to Tomi her favorite response was, "Yeah, even a blind pig finds an acorn every once in awhile." Unworthiness is a story we tell ourselves. Christine Comaford-Lynch, in *Rules for Renegades*, aptly counters this attitude with a new one: "When we're born, we're all given exactly one unit of self-worth. No more, no less. No one can take it away; no one can add to it. Sometimes, though, we've forgotten we have it" (2007, p. 4). If unworthiness is an issue for you, then it is time for you to rediscover your one unit of self-worth. Look in the mirror each morning and declare this choice each morning: "I am worthy!" It is worth repeating here that Canfield's compact disc set *Maximum Confidence: Ten Secrets of Extreme Self-Esteem*, and Maltz and Kennedy's compact disc set *The New-Psycho-Cybernetics: A Mind Technology for Living Your Life Without Limits* are excellent starting points for rediscovering that unit of self worth.

Acknowledging your results is also important to taking action. This step allows us to understand where we are in the creative process. When we *acknowledge* where we are, we discern how close we are to completion of the process or whether the steps we take move us toward our vision. Often times this discernment is referred to as *judgment*. We need to be able to judge where we are so we can acknowledge it. Unfortunately, society has made the word *judgment* negative so Jerry and Tomi prefer the term discernment. Discernment involves a process of assessment rather than a snap decision about something or someone. For this reason, discernment is what leads to acknowledgment. We need acknowledgement to know when we have achieved our vision, completing this round of the creative process.

Intertwined in taking action is recognizing the creative process is messy. Sometimes, it is truly a two step forward, one step backward process. It is never a straight line because we are always course- correcting to get back on track. Besides, the fun is in the journey! Because of the way the creative process functions, perfectionism and fear of failure are constraints on our ability to expand our lives outward. They are structural conflicts. Nobody wants to be a failure so most people have learned not to even try. Perfectionists often don't try, because nothing will ever be good enough. Julia Cameron (2002) so aptly described perfectionism in *The Artist's Way*. She wrote, "Perfectionism is not a quest for the best. It is a pursuit of the worst in ourselves, the part that tells us that nothing we do will ever be good enough—that we should try again" (2002, p. 120).

Perfection and failure are two of the big fences we build around ourselves. "We deny that in order to do something well we must first be willing to do it badly. Instead, we opt for setting our limits at the point where we feel assured of success" (Cameron, p.121). How many times have you said to yourself, "This isn't going to work so I am not even going to try it!"? As you pressure yourself not to fail and to be perfect, remember the flutist or the pianist in the New York Philharmonic didn't just wake up one day, decide to play an instrument, and do so perfectly. Nope. It took years of practice. Just like the bull's-eye is the result of 1000 misses, your great life will be the result of imperfection and setbacks. We will miss the mark sometimes, but we can't get it right if we don't practice.

The stop, drop, and roll strategy that Jerry and Tomi introduced for staying true to your values also works here. As you move toward your vision, each time you take action, or create a new goal, or work toward a goal or an objective, ask yourself, "Is this going to move me forward (closer to my vision)?" If the answer is no, this action does not move you closer to your vision, then you should stop, drop, and roll. Stop and laugh. Drop that action, and roll on to something new. If the answer to this question is continually no, then reassess your vision statement. It might be time to redefine it.

As you look at the results you want to create in your life, it is important to revisit another element of the system and that is the key of *Know the Mental Models*. As discussed in Chapter 3, values are the Mental Model that drive how the Self operates in The Great Life System. If you want to move the Self toward a future state and away from current reality, you must determine if your values are consistent with and support the future state. It might be that your values need to be updated to accomplish the results you seek. To make this determination, complete the Vision-Values Assessment in Figure 18. In order to use this tool, it is best to have available your completed Values Assessment and your Vision Assessment. Take the top five values from your Values Assessment and replace the words Value 1-Value 5 in column one of rows two through six in Figure 18 with each of your five values. Next, answer the question, "Does this value need to be updated to reach the future state in this dimension?" for each value. Use your Vision Assessment to remind yourself of what you seek to create in that dimension.

Value/ Dimension	Self	Family	Faith	Friends	Finances	Fun
Value 1—does this value need to be updated to reach the future state in this dimension?						
Value 2—does this value need to be updated to reach the future state in this dimension?						
Value 3—does this value need to be updated to reach the future state in this dimension?						
Value 4—does this value need to be updated to reach the future state in this dimension?						
Value 5—does this value need to be updated to reach the future state in this dimension?						

Figure 18. Vision - Values Assessment.

If a value needs to be updated to align with your future state or vision, define what the replacement value is. Decide what behaviors align with that value and begin consciously and intentionally choosing to live that way. Also, find a role model who embodies the updated value. Use that person as a reference point for your own behavior.

Finally, to keep your momentum, we recommend you engage in the key of *How to Use the Looking Glass* every six months. By gazing into the mirror to see where you are and where you want to be, you acknowledge where you are and can decide if anything needs re-tooling. At some point, you will reach your future state. Then you can start creating something new based upon what you have already built. The only way to have that knowledge is to continually evaluate the status of your creative process.

In this Chapter Jerry and Tomi shared tools, methods, and strategies for how the Self can candidly see current reality and gain clarity on creating what matters most. By doing so, we begin to see the interplay of the Self with the system and gain insights on the forces that influence the Self. Creativity plays such a large role in achieving the great life. By harnessing the discrepancy between where we are and where we want to be, extraordinary things can happen. In the next Chapter we shift to discussing strategies that help the Self influence the 5Fs.

CHAPTER 6

Key 5: How to Coach the Team

When you take things personally, then you feel offended, and your reaction is to defend your beliefs and create conflicts. You make something big out of something so little, because you have the need to be right and make everyone else wrong.
—*Don Miguel Ruiz*

The fifth and final key to the great life is *How to Coach the Team.* This key offers insights and strategies on how to coach your own gold medal team. This job is not one you can turn down as you have a life time contract to coach this team. That means you can't be fired and you can't quit. Everything rises and falls with you. Of course, you can choose not to actively coach the team, but that leaves you exactly where you are right now, which again raises the question of, "And do you like where that is?" You can continue to coach by default or you can choose to coach by design. Jerry and Tomi recommend coaching by design, because it brings that great life into focus much faster.

Coaching by design incorporates two important elements. First, it means intentionally being a world class coach. Second, it means intentionally creating a world class team to play alongside you. Throughout this Chapter, we will explore both of these concepts and the structural conflict that occurs naturally from functioning in The Great Life System.

To be a world class coach, the Self must operate efficiently and effectively, internally and externally. In the last Chapter, we spent time understanding the internal function of the Self by analyzing whether you saw any of five specific behaviors in your Self. These identified behaviors are indicative of people who don't take responsibility for where they are. To function efficiently and effectively internally, the Self must take responsibility for creating where it is and where it wants to go. Externally, the Self must be an excellent leader for the team. That means avoiding behaviors that can weaken the team.

The external behaviors that can weaken the team are fatal flaws, because they can be such huge barriers to the great life and act as a drag on a coach's overall performance. To understand this concept of fatal flaws for the external Self, we turn to Zenger and Folkman's (2002) research in *The Extraordinary Leader: Turning Good Managers into Great Leaders*. Zenger and Folkman's leadership research indicated that if a leader has a fatal flaw profile, the only course of action is to fix it. The same holds true for you as you coach your team.

Zenger and Folkman (2002) analyzed data from over 200,000 individuals who rated over 25,000 leaders on 360 assessments, a feedback process. Much of their information derived from comparing the attributes and behaviors of the top 10% of leaders with the bottom 10% of leaders. Their research led to an important conclusion: "An analysis of our data reveals five patterns of behavior that consistently lead to a failure in leadership. Possessing one or more of these virtually makes it impossible for a person to be perceived as an effective leader" (Zenger & Folkman, p. 159). These five patterns are:

1. Inability to learn from mistakes.

2. Lack of core interpersonal skills and competencies.

3. Lack of openness to new or different ideas.

4. Lack of accountability.

5. Lack of initiative.

Even though Zenger and Folkman's research uncovered five detrimental behavior patterns, there is one that is considered the single biggest cause of failure: the inability to learn from mistakes. Essentially, all leaders make the same number of mistakes. However, effective leaders use those mistakes as learning experiences while ineffective leaders hide mistakes and then worry about them, sometimes for years. Zenger and Folkman believe this inability to learn from mistakes possibly can be attributed to a leader's failure to see current reality accurately or to be able to analyze one's own behavior. By using the mirror concept explained in Chapters 3 and 5, you can avoid this fatal flaw. The mirror can be used to see current reality more accurately and to see repeating situations that can show patterns of behavior that need to be changed.

Leaders who lack interpersonal skills and competencies limit their overall effectiveness. If you want to be a world class coach, you have to have solid interpersonal skills and competencies. This fatal flaw is easily remedied by reading one of the greatest books ever written on this topic. Jerry and Tomi recommend picking up *How To Win Friends and Influence People* by Dale Carnegie. Carnegie (1982) offers practical tips and advice on how to improve interpersonal skills. Follow his guidance and this fatal flaw profile won't be an issue for you and your gold medal team.

The next fatal flaw is lacking openness to new or different ideas. Leaders who engage in this behavior will do things the same way, because that is the way they have always done them and for no other reason. Tomi's son, Shep, attended a school that loved to use the "but we've always done it that way" excuse. It drove her batty to hear that excuse. Just because something has always been done a certain way doesn't make it right. Leaders who have this profile also tend to be close-minded when it comes to new ideas. To overcome this flaw, ask your team members for their ideas and hear them out. When trying to solve a challenge, ask your teammates this simple question, "What am I missing?" Work to be open-minded and try new things.

Ineffective leaders also don't hold themselves accountable. As the coach of your team, you have to take responsibility for your team and how it functions. Be it good or bad, you must be accountable for the team's performance. If not, you can't build a gold medal team. The best way to begin holding yourself accountable is by asking this question of yourself, "How did my behavior contribute to where we are?" Then make different decisions and act more like the leader you are.

Finally, to be a world class coach, you must have initiative. An ineffective leader is passive and waits for things to happen in order to respond. As the coach of your team, you must make things happen by forging the path. A leader who takes action has a clear picture of current reality and can ask the questions that move the team forward. By engaging in the key of *How to Use the Looking Glass* via the creative process, you take action to understand where you are and where you want to go. If you embody this key, you won't have to worry about lack of initiative showing up in your coaching profile.

An essential element of taking initiative is quiet contemplation. So much static and secondary noise takes place in our lives; sometimes it isn't possible to hear ourselves think. This noise needs to be quieted as there is a powerful connection available to each of us in quiet contemplation that should be an integral part of the great life. This connection has been called gut instinct, sixth sense, intuition, and the mind-heart-soul connection. What the connection is called is irrelevant. What is relevant is the power of using it. We almost always know the solution to a problem, the path to take, or the star to reach for, but the information is hidden deep within. The only way to reach that deep place within is through silence. Each morning or evening, take 10 minutes for yourself and quiet your mind. Focusing on your breathing (think in—out as you breathe) during this time allows you to move away from your cluttered thoughts into quiet contemplation. As you contemplate, take the challenges before you and ask what to do about them. The answer might not come right away, but it will come eventually.

Life requires you to have the right equipment to succeed. You shouldn't play baseball without a glove. Catching a line drive with your bare hand would hurt and might break your hand. You shouldn't eat soup without a spoon. While you could do that, it would be messy, and you might wind up with soup on your shirt. Look at your house, your office, your closet, and your book shelf. Do you have the right equipment to create the great life you want? If you don't, start figuring out what you need, what you can give up, and what needs to be replaced. You want the right equipment for your great life.

As a world-class coach, you should know your playing field, and who is playing on it. This playing field represents all of the dimensions of The Great Life System. You should closely guard who is on your playing field. You do that by selection and deselection of team members. When a coach is picking a team, the first thing he or she is going to do is to assess the current talent with careful consideration (probably with far more consideration than we normally use when deciding on whom to spend our precious time). It's just like try outs from high school: Get a clipboard, write everybody's name down with whom you interact (from your family, circle of friends, and co-workers) and start assessing the talent of your team.

As you go about assessing the talent, keep this one simple rule for being on the team in mind: the player must be dedicated to your success—to moving you forward—in the game of life. As you look at the team member's name, ask the question, "Does this person move me forward?" Either they do or they don't. Either it is a healthy relationship or it isn't. If the person is moving you forward, contributing to your success, or is supporting your dreams, then the person is on your playing team. The people you are spending the most time with should be committed to your happiness and your success. They don't necessarily have to align with your vision or buy into it, but they should be in support of your hopes and dreams.

If there is someone playing on your field who isn't moving you forward, isn't contributing to your success, or isn't supporting your dreams, then as a coach, you need to make the decision to minimize their playing time on your playing field. We call this process deselection, and we categorize these people (who aren't on the playing team) as either benchwarmers or spectators.

Benchwarmers are people you enjoy spending time with, but they may not be supportive of your happiness and success. These people may be bosses, co-workers, or family members with whom you must interact, but they aren't necessarily cheering you on. These people may even be neutral: they aren't moving you forward, but they aren't moving you backward, either.

Spectators are people who you may interact with intermittently, but they have no influence over you. In fact, spectators can yell at you from the bleachers just to let you know they are there, but they are not on your playing field. These people usually have no influence over you or no impact on the daily function of your universe.

Harris (2007), in *The Twelve Universal Laws of Success*, provides a great summary of the importance of knowing where people belong on your team. He calls it "Get Away From The Crowd At The Bottom":

> One of the most difficult steps you will face on your success journey is getting away from the crowd at the bottom. There are many unsuccessful, mediocre people who have failed to recognize, or act on their true potential. If you constantly associate with them, your success journey will be short-lived. You must clear the deck to make room for new associations which will complement and enhance your success efforts.
>
> Once you break away from the mediocre crowd, accept the temporary state of loneliness and prepare for your success. (Harris, 2007, p. 16)

In addition to picking a gold medal team, as the coach you should have a reference point that lives the great life you want. You should seek to model that person's behavior. A reference point acts like a lighthouse during stormy seas or that *permanent whitewater* we talked about in the *Introduction*. Despite all the complexity and chaos taking place, you can always look to your reference point for guidance. Tomi's reference points John Maxwell and Robin Sharma lead exemplary lives dedicated to improving the leadership skills and life skills of people around the globe. They are prolific writers, exceptional public speakers, great thinkers, and live aligned with their values. They represent all the things Tomi aspires to be.

Sometimes our team members and our reference points may not be enough to align us with the great life. Occasionally, we need a cheerleader on our team. A cheerleader can be a mentor, a life coach, a therapist, or a counselor. As we work to transform our lives to the great life, we need a new perspective and someone who cheers for us when others won't or don't. Robin Sharma (2006) offers these words on the impact of having a mentor:

> One of the most effective ways to improve your personal and professional effectiveness and to rise to a new level of excellence is to find a mentor to coach you... A personal coach can illuminate your path,

encourage you when times get tough, and shave years off your learning curve. (p.111)

Find a cheerleader today. You will be amazed at how much this person can help accelerate your travels toward the great life.

One of the most powerful themes on the journey to the great life is courage. We have already discussed areas in which you must exhibit courage. It takes courage to choose to live a great life. It takes courage to look in the mirror to see yourself candidly. It takes courage to stand up for what you truly want to create in this life, even in the face of ridicule from others. It takes courage to stand in the paradox between where you are and what you want to be. It takes courage to embody your values and make them a discipline. It takes courage to be imperfect and to fail. Courage is also mandatory as you coach your team. As part of your great life, you will be called upon to take the following courageous actions:

1. Let go, which includes forgiveness and acceptance.

2. Be rejected.

3. Set personal boundaries (call the penalty when you see it).

4. Make amends.

5. Have authentic conversations.

As you coach your team, you must have the courage to let go of the people and equipment (things) that don't move you forward toward your great life. As Lama Surya Das (2004) observes in *Letting Go of the Person You Used to Be*, "There are many degrees of holding on: daily routines, dogmatic beliefs and prejudices, psychological fixations, phobias, and addictions, are all varieties of holding on" (p. 82). He offers an approach for practicing letting go of people and things to which you feel attached. He suggests practicing letting go in your head: "Experiment in your head with letting go of things you think are important. Let go of one attachment at time. How would your life change?" (p. 74). He suggests asking these questions:

> What would happen, for example, if you gave up the apartment or house you live in and moved into some place smaller or less expensive? Would you need less money to live on and would that make you feel less driven and encumbered? How about most of your clothes and gear...

> How about the people in your life? Is it really true that you can't live without him or her? For just a few minutes, how would it feel to enter-

tain the opposite thought? This is scary, but try it out just for experimental purposes. Say, "I don't need him/her." "I can live without him/her." How does it feel? Try to actually feel and experience that, just for a moment. No outer action is required. (pp. 74-75)

As you go through your list of potential players, recognize that sometimes players need to be benched, traded, or even removed from the team (sent to the bleachers to be a spectator). It is your responsibility to make these decisions as the coach of your team. You must have the courage to make the best decisions for creating a winning team. According to Tommy Newberry (2007), "The dim light of an average life is something we inflict on ourselves" (p. 8). Stop inflicting a life of mediocrity on yourself. Have the courage to do what it takes, whatever it takes, to have your great life.

Throughout their time working with people, Jerry and Tomi have come across three personality profiles that need to be let go from your team right away. As soon as you recognize these types on your team, schedule a trade or make the cut as fast and as *compassionately* as possible. These personality types are the emotional vampire, the drama queen (or king), and the firestarter.

The emotional vampire is negative about everything or is a victim of everything. After this person crosses your path, you might feel like a *Ghostbuster* who has been splatted with green slime. Your next thought is, "Yuck!" If you feel mentally drained or emotionally exhausted after interacting with someone, then they are an emotional vampire.

Drama queens and kings always have something chaotic going on. They want to drag you into the fray and always have an excuse as to why it is not their fault. They are also the "poor, pitiful me" types, demanding your time and creating chaos in your life. They tend to be very powerful personalities, but in all the wrong ways (such as being subtly destructive). These personality types enjoy participating in the drama.

Firestarters are extra special people. They come upon a quiet, serene situation only to start an argument or disagreement. The difference between a firestarter and a drama queen or king is that the firestarter sits back and watches the fireworks they started instead of participating in the drama. Inflammatory comments are their specialty.

In *The Artist's Way*, Cameron (2002) calls these three personality types *crazymakers*. As you assess the talent on your team, identify the emotional vampires, drama queens and kings, firestarters, and crazymakers, and, with a sense of urgency, make a compassionate plan to remove them from your playing field. Your great life should be lived in a drama free zone. Make the choice to live drama free by proclaiming it to the world and then slowly rotating out those team members who create that type of unwanted atmosphere. And, if you suddenly find yourself seated in the bleachers (your friends have taken back their uniforms), you may want to think twice about whether you are a crazymaker.

Jerry and Tomi do not advocate that you wake up tomorrow and decide that everyone on your team has to go. Doing that would be unwise. Instead, we recommend using our *Pick-Off Strategy*. With this strategy, you list and then rank all of the behaviors, people, and equipment (your stuff—cars, home, toys) in your life from healthy to unhealthy. You then take all of the unhealthy behaviors, people, and equipment and rank those from most detrimental to least detrimental. Unhealthy can mean the person doesn't move you forward. Unhealthy can mean owning a piece of equipment that jeopardizes your financial stability (a house or a car you can't afford). You then pick-off the most detrimental. Once you have been able to replace that behavior, friend, or piece of equipment with one that contributes to your great life, pick-off another one. Repeat until there are no more unhealthy behaviors, friends, or equipment on your list.

We recognize that letting go is a difficult process. That is why it takes courage! But, going about the work of your great life means you build a team that is taking you to the championship game. Christine Comaford-Lynch (2007) stresses the importance of surrounding yourself with people who share your goals for self-improvement. She recommends that if you need to let go of a destructive relationship, do so with compassion. Tell that person that he or she is a fine human being. Explain your life is moving in a different direction and it is time for you to move on from this relationship. In fact, any letting go should be done with gentleness, firmness, compassion, and kindness for yourself and for whatever or whomever you are releasing, deselecting, or detaching. How you do it is equally important as why you do it.

There are times when a relationship is destructive, but you are not in a position to let go of it. You want your uniform back, but for whatever reason, that isn't going to happen. That means there is a person on your playing field you want off the team, but you can't make that change because it is a boss, a co-worker, or a family member. If you are faced with this scenario, then spend as little time as possible with that person. Moreover, if minimizing time with that person is not possible, then we suggest using the *Force* as a survival strategy. While this process sounds silly, it really works. Each time you see this person, say in your head, "May the *Force* be with me!" Christine Comaford-Lynch (2007), author of *Rules for Renegades*, suggests you should then activate your deflector shield. Activation is as simple as putting your thumb in your belt loop and pulling on the loop. That way, any of the person's negativity bounces right off of you and is diffused throughout the container that holds your personal universe. Anytime Tomi has to go on to a person's playing field who is a crazymaker, she puts her shield up. It totally changes the mindset about spending time on this person's playing field because Tomi now takes the position that this person can't say or do anything that impacts her.

If the deflector shield doesn't help you with the crazymakers, then you may implement another strategy we call *AfterTalk*. *AfterTalk* is one of the practices of the great life that's easy to implement. In fact, it's a lot of fun. Many times, because we don't have a ready list of comebacks or retorts to the hurtful or spiteful comments of others, we fall back into old habits or *shenpa*, and usually react in old ways that likely escalate the situation or leave you or the other person feeling bad or hurt. *AfterTalk* changes that. It is a list of possible one-liners that give you the opportunity to shift old thinking to new thinking after someone says something to you that causes a reaction in you. What do we mean by a reaction or *shenpa*?

Tomi was introduced to *shenpa* by Pema Chödron, an American Buddhist nun, through her compact disc set *Getting Unstuck*. According to Chödron,

> *Shenpa* is the urge, the hook, that triggers our habitual tendency to close down…
>
> Someone criticizes you. They criticize your work or your appearance or your child. At moments like that, what is it you feel? It has a familiar taste in your mouth, it has a familiar smell… The Tibetan word for this is *shenpa*… When *shenpa* hooks us, we're likely to get stuck… It's an everyday experience. Even a spot on your new sweater can take you there. At the subtlest level, we feel a tightening, a tensing, a sense of closing down. Then we feel a sense of withdrawing, not wanting to be where we are… That tight feeling has the power to hook us into self-denigration, blame, anger, jealousy and other emotions which lead to words and actions that end up poisoning us… Yet we don't stop—we can't stop—because we're in the habit of associating whatever we're doing with relief from our own discomfort. This is the *shenpa* syndrome. The word "attachment" doesn't quite translate what's happening. It's a quality of experience that's not easy to describe but which everyone knows well.

Shenpa draws us into old patterns of behavior that have yet to work for us. But, with the tool of *AfterTalk*, we can stop the *shenpa*.

How is *AfterTalk* best used? Here is an example. You have a colleague at work who puts your dreams down. Today, you share with her you would like to take a summer vacation in Fiji. Her response, "You will never save enough money to do that. You spend too much money on frivolous things." Your typical response might be, "Susie, that's not true. I don't buy a lot of frivolous stuff." Your statement usually leads to a round robin of disagreeable comments, sniping, and both people walk away hurt. Rather than a typical response where ego kicks in to defend, use an *AfterTalk* like, "Let's admire that problem," "That's changing," "Keep that up and you may get voted off the island," or "My bank account is growing!" We have provided a list of suggested *AfterTalk* in Figure 19.

It's a great life!	I am blowing the whistle on that one!	I am going to have to throw a flag at this point!
Calgon take me away!	Pressure is a privilege!	Undefend enough to hear me out.
I want my uniform back.	I'm going to need some spinach for this!	This is not the hill I am prepared to die on!
I'm just holding the mirror.	With great power comes great responsibility!	Today's failures are tomorrow's successes.
Talk me off the ledge.	Some will. Some won't.	Want to reconsider that?
There's a meditation for that.	That's changing!	Take the steam out of that.
It's in the bag!	Can we pause here	Hit the reset button!
Go big or go home!	Oh, my, what a shank!	It's not an argument, it's a recognition.
You lucky dog!	I'm still growing!	Let's admire that problem.
That's real funny!	Ask your mama!	When you are in a hole stop digging.
In your dreams!	Next week!	Do you have it or does it have you?
That's so beautiful.	Oh, really!	I'd rather eat broken glass.
I'm so beautiful.	I am lovable and capable.	I see signs of occupational maturity!
You're so beautiful.	Get out?!?	I am great just as I am.
First class, baby!	Why not!	Show me the money!
Whoa there missy, put on some brakes!	Say what?	Snap!
It's in the past.	I'm done.	My bank account is growing!
That's the bomb.	Show me.	That is so clever!
That's the ticket.	I like it.	Don't try this at home!
I love it!	Gotta have it.	That's so clever!

Get your own.	Good stuff.	That's not me.
That's what I'm talkin' about!	That'll work.	Has someone died here?
In a jiffy!	Flip it.	It's an insight, not an insult.
What would J.C. do?	What would Buddha do?	The best is yet to be.
Why not?	Thank you for releasing me from that prison!	Stop running from things that aren't chasing you.
When pigs fly!	Hadn't seen it on Oprah yet so it can't be true.	That's a really good watch out!
How's that working for you?	Dr. Phil didn't say that.	We need an intervention.
The sun will still rise tomorrow.	Creativity is messy.	Let's give that distance before jumping in.
Okay, I'll bite.	Keep that up and you may get voted off the island!	I'm not touching that.
Do you think that's close to delusional?	Door closes, window opens.	You asked for it so no complaints will be accepted.
Amplify that.	You little instigator!	This is a drama free zone!

Figure 19. AfterTalk.

These *AfterTalk* statements are designed to be said with humor and gentleness. They are intended to shift the tone and energy of the moment to something more positive and constructive, and hopefully, evoke some laughter. *AfterTalk* is not intended to hurt someone's feelings or cause pain. As you go about the work of your great life, any task, exercise, process, or learning is completed with compassion and kindness for everyone!

Why develop *AfterTalk*? Because too often we allow our egos to waste so much time and vital energy attempting to be right or fighting over things that don't really matter. By using *AfterTalk*, we shift our reaction to a more positive one. It helps us to avert that hooked and sinking feeling of *shenpa* that compels us to expend energy on something that is unimportant. What do we mean by something *unimportant*? Well, in actuality almost everything is unimportant. In fact, Tomi once read the only things that matter are the time of birth and the time of death; everything else is irrelevant. If we only lived that way, we could save so much of our energy for more important things.

Tomi has a personal story on determining what is important. In the winter of 2008, Jerry and Tomi's family suffered two catastrophic events. Their mother, Janie, and brother, Mike, were both gravely ill. Due to their constant healthcare needs and the seriousness of their illnesses, Tomi invited them to live with her. Janie and Mike spent most of their time arguing with each other in Tomi's living room. During this time, Tomi was able to see how we get sucked into problems, dilemmas, and crises that aren't even ours. And, it all starts when we open our mouths. This scenario hammered home the adage of listen more, talk less.

As Tomi witnessed Janie and Mike's constant bickering (and because they were in the living room of her house, it wasn't possible to escape), she realized they argued over inconsequential affairs. What was remarkable was how emotionally charged Janie and Mike became over that small stuff because each of them wanted to be right. Their actions led Tomi to enter into a silent period of less words and more thought. She decided there are really only two things that must be said in life: "I love you," and "Watch out for that cliff!" (Or, use an equivalent safety phrase.) So, when Mom and Mike went at it, Tomi said, "Hey, quit the bickering. There are only two things you need to say to each other and they are 'I love you' and 'Watch out for that cliff'. Everything else is superfluous!" If matters don't intrude on your playing field or they don't impact your path to the great life, then don't get involved. When Tomi sees that one of her sons is emotionally charged about something, one of the first things she will ask is, "Hey, is that on your playing field? If not, then let it go."

Other great authors, philosophers, and spiritualist have written about the importance of recognizing what matters. Eckart Tolle (2006) shared the following anecdote about J. Krishnamurti, the great Indian philosopher and spiritual teacher, who spoke and traveled all over the world for more than 50 years:

> At one of the talks in the later part of his life, he surprised his audience by asking, "Do you want to know my secret?" Everyone became very alert. Many people in the audience had been coming to listen to him for twenty or thirty years and still failed to grasp the essence of his teaching. Finally, after all these years, the master would give them the key to understanding. "This is my secret," he said. "I don't mind what happens." (p. 198)

Teach yourself to not mind what happens. Don't become attached to the outcome. One of Tomi's favorite lines when someone attempts to drag her into matters that aren't pertinent to her playing field is, "Thanks for sharing that, but I am not invested in what happens." Another favorite line of Tomi's is, "Oh, isn't that interesting!"

Robin Sharma (2008) offered this approach in *The Greatness Guide*: "A question I sometimes ask myself when I'm facing a struggle is this one: 'Will this matter a year from now?' If not, I move on --fast" (p. 186). Sharma also asks, "Has someone died here?" (p. 186). If the answers are no, stop renting space to that matter in your head.

The point of *AfterTalk* is to shift us to the, "I don't mind what happens," and the "Will this matter a year from now?" mindset. It allows us to choose to be happy and at peace rather than expend energy engaging in an ego battle of who is right over something that is irrelevant to the great life path. Jack Canfield (2007) has a pearl of wisdom on this issue in his *Maximum Confidence: Ten Secrets of Extreme Self-Esteem*, noting it doesn't matter who is right, what matters is what is right!

Bishop Jordan (2007), in *The Laws of Thinking*, emphasizes the need to be able to walk away. Doing so "means that you must have the insight and depth of discernment to choose your goals and leave behind the things and people that are not your goals or do not serve your goals" (p.156). Maybe it's being able to say "no" to a raucous night out with friends, because you know you have to lead a team through a huge project at work the next day. Maybe it's being able to shift a person from your playing team to the bench or from the bench to the bleachers. Taking these actions means you have mastered that problem. "If you can walk away from a thing or a person, you can let it go. It no longer has power over you; you have power over it" (Jordan, 2007, p. 157). One of Tomi's favorite lines when she sees her children grappling with an issue is, "Do you have *it* or does *it* have you?" So many times *it* has us!

Eckart Tolle (2008) offers a fitting zen monk parable about letting go. Two zen monks, one old and one young, were walking along a country road that had become extremely muddy after the rains. Near a village, the monks came upon a young woman who was trying to cross the road, but the mud was so deep it would have ruined her silk kimono. The elder of the two monks picked up the young woman and carried her to the other side of the road. The monks then continued walking in silence. Five hours later, as they approached the lodging temple, the younger monk couldn't restrain himself any longer. He asked the older monk, "Why did you carry that girl across the road? You know we monks are not supposed to touch women." The older monk responded, "I put that girl down hours ago. Why are you still carrying her around?"

What girl are you still carrying around that you can put down today?

A conflict in which people often find themselves embroiled as they move toward their great life is friends and family who try to anchor them to the same spot. Others don't want you to transform. As you march toward your great life that means the people in your life either have to begin their march forward, too, or be left behind. Because most people are comfortable where they are, they don't want to move forward, and they certainly don't want to be left behind. Consequently, these friends and family try to disrupt your progress toward the great life. In *The Artist's Way*, Cameron (2002) describes what to be on the look-out for from friends and family: "Be particularly alert to any suggestion that you have become selfish or different. (These are red-alert words for us. They are attempts to leverage us back into our old ways for the sake of someone else's comfort, not our own.)" (p. 43). Recognize these comments as attempts to ground you in somebody else's current reality. Don't fall prey to the potential impact of such statements: the letting go of your vision.

Tomi vividly remembers an ugly conversation she had with her mother, Janie, on this very issue. As Tomi went about the work of creating her great life, she could clearly see she was moving away from some members of her family. So could those family members. In the moment, neither Tomi nor Janie understood what was taking place. Since neither of them could explain what they were feeling, emotions abounded. Janie told Tomi she was so selfish (one of Cameron's buzz words). Janie was emotional and upset with Tomi, almost yelling at her. Tomi wasn't all that pleasant in her response. Superficially, the conversation looked like a disagreement between mother and daughter. At a deeper level, Janie wanted Tomi to stay in the same place, and Tomi didn't want to stay in the same place. If you are the person trying to move forward, have compassion for those who are being left behind. Many times, those being left behind don't know how to voice their discomfort or may not even be aware of why they are upset. However, you are aware, and your best response is to answer any claim of "you're selfish" or "you're different" with this simple response: "I can see why you might feel that way." Identifying with the other person's feelings helps diffuse the resistance. Besides, there is no need to engage in a family brawl over the work of creating your great life. Tomi just wishes she knew that three years ago!

As part of setting boundaries, it is so important to teach people how to treat you. Many times when others offend or hurt us, we don't say anything. We don't call the penalty, blow our imaginary whistle, or throw our imaginary red flag. Instead, we walk away licking our wounds and telling others of our hurt. As we tell others of our hurt or of the offense, we continue to build a story around it. As the story builds, we become entrenched in the story, and we identify with those emotions. All wrong! The moment the offense takes place, stand up for yourself. It is so important to have the courage to call the penalty when it happens. Yes, in addition to being the coach of the team, you also have to be the referee. Many people behave rudely or inappropriately, because we allow it. Don't allow it. Call the penalty by telling the person what they just did was offensive or hurt your feelings. Ask them not to do it again. If the person persists in that hurtful or offensive behavior, then they don't need to be on your playing field. Have the courage to minimize the time you spend on their field or the time you allow them to be on yours.

Another conflict occurs from lack of understanding. More people would let go, if they only knew what to let go of! In *The Artist's Way*, Cameron (2002) suggests writing each morning about anything and everything. She calls these morning pages. She says hidden within the writings of the morning pages are the things we need to let go of. If writing morning pages isn't attractive to you, another method for uncovering what needs to be released is offered below in the section on forgiveness. Regardless of the method chosen, the goal is too truthfully examine what is not working in your life. Investigate and scrutinize what is operating as a block to moving forward and let go of those things.

Letting go also means releasing past hurts. Dwelling on past hurts gives those events power over you. It is like renting space in your head to unproductive thoughts and emotions. These hurts are energy leaks in your life force, diverting precious energy away from what really matters. Forgiveness frees that space in your head for more important great life activities. Jack Kornfield (2004), in *The Art of Forgiveness, Lovingkindness and Peace*, through the dialogue between two former prisoners of war, offers a compelling example of how our own refusal to forgive keeps us captive:

> First former prisoner of war: "Have you forgiven your captors yet?"
>
> Second former prisoner of war: "No, never!"
>
> First former prisoner of war: "Well, then, they still have you in prison, don't they?" (p. 22)

Who still has you imprisoned because you won't forgive them?

Forgiveness is the pathway to peace:

> Forgiveness is about acceptance. Forgiveness can't erase all hurt, and that's just the way things are sometimes. We accept our sadness and our wounds. But, it's our choice whether we let that hurt control us, or if we acknowledge it, and then let it go. Letting it go is the only way to reclaim the peace in our lives. (Cordova, 2003, p. 51)

To forgive is to let go of the emotional baggage we carry around with us every day. And, it is so freeing! When Tomi started working on her great life, she went on a self-improvement weekend retreat. During the weekend she participated in a forgiveness ceremony. As part of this ceremony, Tomi had to find a partner so they could share with each other what they were angry and mad about. They had to hold hands and look each other in the eye as they revealed inner secrets. Tomi was amazed at what came out of her mouth during this ceremony. Here is what she said:

> I am angry at my brother for continuing to drink and ruin every family event for the last 10 years. I am mad at my mother for not being more sophisticated. I am mad because I can't play volleyball anymore. I am angry because I said I would never be heavy like my mother and here I am overweight, just like my mother. I am mad at my dad for not getting regular medical attention. I am mad at God for taking my Dad, my Aunt, and my Uncle so quickly. I hate cancer! I am mad, disappointed, angry, and frustrated at my father for not taking better care of his money.

When Tomi announced these hurts she had unconsciously been renting space to in her head, she felt such relief at letting go of these secrets. After making these statements, Tomi and her partner had to say these words to each other: "I forgive you. I forgive me. You forgive you. You forgive me. I forgive my mother and my father. I forgive my family and my friends. I forgive everybody." Tomi felt so much lighter, emotionally and physically. When Tomi got back home to North Carolina, after several days of reflection, she realized she had let go of a lifetime of hurts and anger. Forgiving was so freeing.

Tomi thought the forgiveness ceremony might be helpful for her mom, Janie. To Tomi it seemed like Janie had a lifetime of built-up anger she needed to get off her back. Shortly after returning home, Tomi sat down with Janie and said, "Mom, let's have a forgiveness ceremony." She said, "What if I don't want to forgive?" Tomi responded with, "Mom, why would you not want to forgive?" At that time Tomi didn't understand. Janie's anger and resentment were part of her identity. She had made them part of who she is. She became her emotions. If she let go of the anger and forgave, she feared losing a piece of herself. Tomi just moved to the next questions: "Mom, who are you angry at? Who do you need to forgive?" Janie said, "I am still mad at your Uncle Herbert." Uncle Herbert is Jerry and Tomi's uncle who had been deceased for over 30 years when this conversation occurred. "What?" Tomi exclaimed, "Mom, he's been dead about 30 years; how can you still be mad at him?" All she said was "Well, I still am."

Tomi just looked at Janie with great curiosity and finally said, "Mom, I don't think this is going to work for you right now." That ended the conversation. Tomi was stunned to realize how long and how deeply humans are capable of harboring hurts. Such unforgiving behavior leads nowhere. What Tomi since learned is that she should have said this to her mother, "Okay, mom. I understand you are still angry. Why not just forgive yourself for not being ready to forgive." Even though we don't forgive the person that is the subject of our ire, this approach still starts the letting go process. As you reflect upon your anger, frustration, or disappointment, and as you work to forgive, if you can't, it is okay. Instead, forgive yourself for not being ready to forgive.

Once we scrape away pieces of our karmic scrap heap, it is important to keep ourselves from accumulating another karmic scrap heap. An ideal way to do so is to take the time at the end of the day to write down all the slights you felt during the day. Anything that made you angry, mad, frustrated or disappointed, write it down. Tomi used to write her slights in her *Letting Go Journal*. Once her slights from the day are released on paper, she says a forgiveness mantra: "I forgive everyone, and I ask that everyone forgive me. And, so it is." If you commit to this practice at the end of each day, you are cleansing your mind so you don't rent space in your head to things that don't really matter. If this method doesn't work for you, try Cameron's morning pages.

Letting go is also about acceptance. In order to live the great life, we must accept our current reality. We must see exactly where we are and quit arguing with reality or struggling against the tide. In *Let Go, Let Miracles Happen*, Cordova (2003) defines acceptance as "letting go of our expectations about how things *should* be and appreciating what is" (p. 47). When we stop struggling, we can get into the flow of life.

As part of coaching your team, you must have the courage to set and honor your personal boundaries. Tomi has worked through a lot of people and experiences on her way to the great life. One of those people was an enormously helpful coach named Mack Arrington. Arrington regularly sends out an e-mail newsletter entitled *Life by Design, Not by Default* to current and past clients. His December 1, 2008 newsletter had a perfect example of why it is important to set personal boundaries:

Get the Distinction: Toleration vs. Tolerance

A *toleration* is something you put up with. A *tolerance* is the range of what you put up with. Tolerations can be very, VERY, expensive in terms of time, money and other resources. For example, you might tolerate someone who calls you once a week and talks for 20 minutes, but if they start calling for 20 minutes every day, your tolerance might be overstepped pretty quickly.

Tolerations can include people, things, situations, problems, stress, too much/too little, rules, clutter, disorganization, communication, career, technology, equipment, money, relationships, etc. - plus time you waste just thinking about it can be a toleration.

We want to eliminate tolerations or at least reduce the range of what you tolerate. For example, eliminating a toleration for someone who calls you every day for 20 minutes saves you two workweeks a year (240 days x 20 minutes = 4,800 minutes = 80 hours = two weeks). Of course, eliminating a 20-minute phone toleration with your supervisor or in-laws might not be in your best interest… but sometimes you can make points by being more organized and attentive and thus shorten the calls.

Are there tolerations you can easily eliminate like taking care of home repairs or buying the new equipment? Are there other tolerations—perhaps business related or relationships, that take more planning and time to change? How will you plan and implement the changes you need to make?

A first-rate but outrageous example of having the courage to live within your personal boundaries is provided by Sheldon from CBS's television show *The Big Bang Theory*. One episode centers on Sheldon's idiosyncrasies. Sheldon, his roommate, and two friends are well schooled in Sheldon's "three strikes and you are out" approach (unless of course you take Sheldon's class and then the strikes are wiped clean). The next-door neighbor, Penny, engages in behavior, in quick succession, that amounts to three Sheldon strikes. She is then out! The remainder of the episode is about how Penny tries to get back in Sheldon's good graces without taking his class (even though Penny is implored to please take the class). While the behavior Penny engaged in was mild and included touching Sheldon's food and sitting in his seat, the point of the episode was not lost on Jerry and Tomi. Sheldon had a discipline about the way he lived and what his teammates could and could not do on his playing field. He knew what his personal boundaries were, and he made a discipline out of living by them. In other words, he was willing to call a penalty on his friends when he saw it. His friends honored that discipline, and if they didn't, they were off the team.

It is important to stress that even though Sheldon was clear about his personal boundaries, he was willing to forgive. If you took his class, he would let you back on the team. Our boundaries would be so much easier to honor if we were more demonstrative about them in our lives. What are you tolerating in your life that needs *picking-off*? What behaviors are "three strikes and you are out" for you? What puts a person in the penalty box? If we don't know the answers to these questions, then we can't enforce our own personal boundaries.

Often we delay enforcing our boundaries, because we worry about hurting someone's feelings. We might live in fear that enforcing our boundaries might mean someone will stop liking us or stop loving us. Or worse yet, someone might abandon us. Tomi had such an experience. Unfortunately, she allowed herself to be pushed to the edge of a breakdown before she decided to have the courage to hold her ground. The experience is shared below and is lengthy. The detail shows how long it took Tomi to learn the lesson!

By the time Tomi was ready to learn her lesson on having the courage to set her boundaries, Janie and Mike had lived in her living room (except when in the hospital) for over four months. Already Mike had been near death twice with two extended hospitalizations. Shortly after he was first admitted to the hospital, Tomi was in Mike's room when one of his treating physicians dropped in to check on him. Tomi introduced herself to the doctor and asked about Mike's status because she had not seen much improvement in the first three days of hospitalization. The doctor then shared Mike's diagnosis with Tomi: "Your brother has pneumonia, *e coli*, and catastrophic liver failure." In Tomi's mind she thought, "This can't be good." So Tomi asked the deadly follow-up question, "So what is his prognosis?" The doctor looked at Tomi stiffly and said, "Can I be honest with you?" Tomi replied, "Sure, I wouldn't expect anything less." The doctor explained, "I have seen people with your brother's liver function studies die in less than a few weeks. If he survives, your brother will either need a TIPS procedure or a liver transplant. He can never drink again." Tomi knew what a liver transplant was but she had to ask about the TIPS procedure. It is when a shunt is placed in the liver to help fluid bypass the liver, because the liver is so compromised it can't process all of the bodily fluids being sent to it.

While Mike was on another plane, lost between here and the hereafter, Janie was enduring multiple surgeries to correct a kidney ailment. While Mike was in the hospital in Greensboro, Tomi often had Janie in the hospital in Winston Salem. By the time Mike was stabilized near the end of April, Janie had undergone the first two surgeries in the series of three, plus a repeat of surgery number two. The purpose of the second surgery was to remove any kidney stones and brush the kidney (whatever that means). Essentially, as Tomi understood all of the medical jargon being thrown at her, the kidney was being cleaned out and prepped for the final surgery. But what no one told Tomi was that Janie would come home from that second surgery with two tubes sticking out of her kidney, draining into a urine bag. The family (meaning Tomi) was not properly advised on the care of these bags or Janie's wound. Janie leaked urine all over the furniture in the house (anything she sat in, or on, or laid down on). It was at that point Tomi seriously considered buying stock in the company that makes Febreeze! For weeks the Bryan house smelled awful. First, it smelled of urine from those awful bags Janie had to carry around. Tomi could only imagine how Janie felt about those bags, as Janie could never retreat from the smell. Second, the house smelled of old bandages because Mike still had his chest tube in that drained infection into a box that was attached to the tube. The box, which could not be cleaned, was entering its sixth week of holding infection. It was ripe, to say the least. Mike began to wrap the box in multiple layers of plastic bags but that odor was strong, and it had no trouble permeating the three layers of plastic. Tomi affectionately began to refer to Mike as infection bucket and to Mom as pee bag. She would come into the house and yell, "Hey, pee bag and infection bucket, what is going on?" Tomi is not sure Mike and Janie thought it was as funny as she did, but Tomi was trying to make light of what was a dire situation. At one point, the smell became so bad in the house that Mike began burning incense in an effort to cover up the foul odors.

At one point, Tomi thought, "Goodness gracious, could this get any worse?" Her mother Janie had to walk around with a pee bag! Everywhere Tomi went the infection bucket and pee bag had to go. That urine bag set up was bad news. It got to the point where Tomi had to place large plastic trash bags over Janie's bed so the mattress wouldn't get drenched with urine. Tomi also placed a big trash bag over a chair in the living room that Janie liked to sit in. That was about the only chair Tomi allowed her to sit in. Later, when Janie moved out of the Bryan house that chair went to the dump!

Jim, Tomi, Shep, and Warren's lives were disrupted by caring for Mike with his life threatening medical condition and by caring for Janie with her extreme kidney ailment. Add to that mix the revolving door of relatives (and there were many) over five months and the situation got even more interesting. It really was a doctors, nurses, and sick people on parade kind of thing. Through it all, and Tomi means all (changing bandages, ER visits, odiferous wounds, chest tubes, wound vacuums, surgeries, and decisions to burn furniture because we never wanted to sit in it again after *that* happened to it), she smiled and was a gracious host to whomever crossed her threshold.

But, the rubber band known as Tomi Bryan's life was stretched about as thin as it could be. She had been setting no boundaries for herself so the universe kept piling on. And, the next load of karmic scrap was going to make it all very interesting.

Janie had her last surgery on Thursday, May 3, 2008. On Friday, May 9, the hospital staff advised Tomi that Janie would be released the next day. Great! Janie would be back in the living room on Dover Road on Sunday, May 11 for a Mother's Day celebration. Since Mike was feeling better, and Jerry was visiting from Idaho, Janie would have three of her children together for Mother's Day. What a treat for her. Later that same Friday, Tomi received a call from a nurse asking if she would mind being responsible for changing Janie's bandage once she got home. Tomi said, "Hey, as long as all I have to do is change a bandage, I am okay with that." On Friday, Janie and Tomi agreed that Janie would call Tomi when she was ready to be discharged. At that point, Jerry would ride to Winston Salem and pick Janie up. Tomi couldn't make the pick up, because her youngest son, Warren, was playing in a tennis tournament, and she wanted to watch him play. The challenge with sending Jerry to pick up Janie rested with Jerry's own physical illness. At the time Jerry was taking 11 blood pressure medications and was under strict doctor's orders to limit his activities. Thus, picking up Janie would be Jerry's one activity for the day.

Around 2:00 p.m. on Saturday Jerry gets the call that Janie is ready. When he arrived at the hospital, the discharge nurse started reviewing Janie's medical needs. When Jerry heard the description of his and Tomi's responsibilities, he stopped the conversation with a, "You are going to have to call my sister. I don't think she is going to do all that." Tomi is at the tennis tournament happily watching Warren play when her cell phone vibrates. She sees it is Jerry, so she answers. Jerry launches right in, "You won't believe want they want us to do for mom. They want us to pack her wound and I told them they had to talk to you, because I didn't think you would want to do this." As Tomi listened, she thought here we go again. "Jerry, it can't be all that bad?" His quick response was, "Oh, yes, it is!" Tomi then heard him say to someone, "Here, you tell my sister what you want us to do." Then, Tomi heard a female voice, "Hi, this is the discharge nurse for your mom. We are instructing your brother on how to change your mom's bandage, and he said I needed to tell you." Tomi said, "Okay, tell me what we have to do." What Tomi heard come through the telephone amazed her. The nurse said, "Everyday you will need to repack this wound. You will cut a three foot strip of gauze and soak it in saline solution. While it is soaking, pull the old gauze out of the wound" and before she could say another word Tomi growled, "Stop right there. You have to be kidding me. That is not changing a bandage. That is minor surgery. I am already taking care of a brother who just two days ago had a chest tube pulled out. The brother you are looking at is on 11 different blood pressure medications. He gets to do one thing a day and since you are looking at him, this is his one thing. I am not adding to that packing a wound. I am sorry, I can't. Unless you can have home health care at the house for her today she is not coming home. You either keep her or find a short term stay place for her. I just can't add that to my list." When Tomi stopped the tirade, the nurse said "Okay, we will see what we can do." Jerry got back on the line, and Tomi told him that he was not to bring Janie home. He said all right. Tomi also told Jerry to tell Janie that we love her and our refusal to bring her home had nothing to do with our love for her and had everything to do with our inability to properly care for her. Later, Tomi called Janie to make sure she was okay with the decision not to bring her home. She said she understood, and it was not a problem.

Throughout Operation Janie and Mike, Tomi was like the Energizer Bunny. She just kept going and going. Whatever it was, she would do it. Emergency Room at 9:00 p.m.? No problem. Two family members, each with a surgery in different cities on the same day? Tomi can manage that. Tomi felt compelled to do it all, because if she said no, someone might not love her anymore. Tomi approached a nervous breakdown from being overwhelmed by two sick people living in her living room and by keeping track of all the medicines and doctor appointments.

And, on this particular Saturday, when she felt like she was being asked to take on an even bigger burden, there was a terrible war raging inside of Tomi. Tomi thought, "Mom will be mad if I don't bring her home. She will stop loving me. I will be a bad daughter for leaving Mom at the hospital over Mother's Day." The battle was escalating when the voice of reason finally broke free. From deep inside, Tomi heard, "Tomi, you are not trained as a nurse. You don't have to be responsible for this. Stand up for yourself and just say no. It will all be okay." So, Tomi told that discharge nurse no and guess what? Tomi's mother still loved her. Tomi's brothers and husband supported her decision. What a revelation. Tomi could maintain her personal space and still be accepted and loved. Tomi didn't have to overdo it to keep the affections of others. She recognized that people will love you even if you can't bring the dessert for Friday night's party or be the committee chair. And, if they do stop loving you because you say no, then you don't need them on your playing field.

Tomi ignored her own needs and those needs of her husband, her children, and her business to run Operation Janie and Mike. Because Tomi wouldn't say no (she was busy trying to be a good daughter and a good sister), and failed to establish any personal boundaries, the universe kept piling on. It was almost as if the universe was chuckling and saying, "Let's see how much more she is oblivious enough to take!" If Tomi looked in the mirror during this time, she may have seen the repeating pattern of being dumped on. From there, she could have asked, "Why does this keep happening?" It kept happening because Tomi would not set limits. As the coach of the team you must have the courage to set your personal boundaries with your players. Tomi didn't establish her boundaries and it almost cost her. The price would have been her own well-being. Don't allow piling on. Call that penalty when you see it. Throw the flag and stop the game. You have to, because your great life requires it.

As the coach of your team, it is your game and you get to make the rules. So make them! What are the penalties on your playing field? Jerry and Tomi suggest you spend time deciding what those are.

Sometimes players make the choice to leave a team. As a coach, you have to have the courage to accept rejection with grace. There are four important practices that help us to gracefully accept rejection. Two of these practices come from Comaford-Lynch's (2007) *Rules for Renegades*. First, Comaford-Lynch advises subscribing to the rock rejection mantra: Some will. Some won't. So what? Someone's waiting. If someone wants off the team, let them go. If you try to hold a person on your team with the use of force or manipulation, that team member may lose their desire to move you forward.

Tomi recently had the privilege of hearing Mike Eruzione speak. Eruzione captained the 1980 United States Olympic Hockey Team to a gold medal. As captain of the team, Eruzione certainly learned what it takes to assemble a gold medal team and the discipline required to be a champion. One of the points he made during his speech was, "If you don't want to be here, don't show up." If someone doesn't want to be on your gold medal team, don't make them show up. If you don't want to be on someone's team, don't show up. Showing up with a bad attitude moves no one forward.

The second practice from Comaford-Lynch (2007) is to use the *Quit Taking It Personally* (QTIP) method. If someone doesn't want to be on your team, let them go and QTIP. One of the agreements in Don Miguel Ruiz's (1997) *The Four Agreements* is to not take anything personally. Ruiz says:

> As you make a habit of not taking anything personally, you won't need to place your trust in what others do or say. You will only need to trust yourself to make responsible choices. You are never responsible for the action of others; you are only responsible for you. When you truly understand this, and refuse to take things personally, you can hardly be hurt by the careless comments or action of others.
>
> If you keep this agreement, you can travel around the world with your heart completely open and no one can hurt you. You can say, "I love you," without fear of being ridiculed or rejected. You can ask for what you need. You can say yes, or you can say no—whatever you choose—without guilt or self-judgment. You can choose to follow your heart always. Then you can be in the middle of hell and still experience inner peace and happiness. You can stay in your state of bliss, and hell will not affect you at all. (pp. 60-61)

When you come to the realization that you are fine just as you are, your personal power skyrockets. You can be and do anything you want without fear of criticism, reprisal, rejection, or failure. You make decisions and choices based on what you want and not what others think. It is a powerful moment to face and accept this realization.

The third way for managing rejection comes from Canfield's (2007) *Maximum Confidence: Ten Secrets of Extreme Self-Esteem*. Canfield advises that when you don't get what you want, say something positive to yourself. One such comment might be, "That's great. There must be something better in store for me around the corner!" The fourth way is an old Quaker philosophy of saying to yourself "Door closes, window opens." Sometimes the greatest things happen to us because we didn't get what we originally wanted. Be happy about rejection, because it means something grander and better is waiting.

A coach must have the courage to make amends. There might be a spectator you really want in your bleachers or on your playing team, but somehow you offended that person. Now, they don't talk to you. They don't return your telephone calls, text messages, or e-mails. The best way to resolve this dilemma is to make amends. When you make amends, you correct a perceived wrong. If you don't know how to do this, then just say to the person, "I messed up. What can I do to make it up to you?"

If there are people in your life you need to apologize to, then Jerry and Tomi recommend making an Amends Plan. This plan identifies those people to whom you need to make amends. The plan also maps out what you will say and the timeline for completing these amends. A sample plan is shown in Figure 20.

Person	Script	Timeline
Sherry	Sherry, I apologize for not standing up for you last year when the boss said you didn't deliver. I know it wasn't your fault. I know that cost you a bonus and that was wrong of me. I hope you can forgive me.	By June 16
Karl	Karl, I am sorry that I just shut you out of my life without explanation but I was scared and I did not know what else to do. I realize that was wrong. I would like to open the door between us. Can you tell me how to do that?	By July 15

Figure 20. Amends Plan.

It is nice to believe that everyone to whom you are making amends will accept your words. That is not always the case. Sometimes people like to hold onto the drama or the story they created around the hurt so they won't let go of the perceived hurt you may have caused. Just remember the rock rejection mantra—either they will or they won't. If someone doesn't want to make amends with you, you can't make them. All you can do is offer, and then it is what it is.

Last, but by no means least, as coach of your team, you must be willing to have authentic conversations with everyone—those on your playing field, bench-warmers, and those sitting in the bleachers. An authentic conversation is when you stand in your truth, speak from the heart, and say what needs to be said without drama or pretext. It is when you say what needs to be said with compassion and empathy. Author Susan Scott (2004) calls these fierce conversations. She says, "A fierce conversation is one in which we come out from behind ourselves into the conversation and make it real" (2004, p. 7). Her philosophy on the topic of conversation is a great one:

> You are an original, an utterly unique human being. You cannot have the life you want, make the decisions you want, or be the leader you are capable of being until your actions represent an authentic expression of who you really are, or who you wish to become. (2004, p. 67)

Jerry and Tomi believe Scott (2004) provides an excellent explanation of the coach's role in the authentic conversation:

> During a fierce conversation, my role is not to say what is easy to say or what we all can say, but to say what we have been unable to say. I try to pay attention to things that may pass unobserved by others and bring them out into the open. The most valuable thing any of us can do is find a way to say the things that can't be said. (p. 174)

As the coach of your team, you must have authentic and fierce conversations. You have to say what needs to be said. You have to call the penalty. You have to lead the way. You have to inspire. You have to believe. And, you can only do those things when you come out from behind yourself and make it real.

There is one last practice Jerry and Tomi recommend you engage in as coach. At the end of a season, a great coach reevaluates the talent on his or her team. This is the time when players get promoted, traded, cut, or benched. As the coach of your team, you must also annually evaluate the status of the team and its equipment. Revisiting these decisions allows you to continue to practice the discipline of moving forward, marching toward your great life.

All of these practices result in one thing for the world-class coach: a complete life. A complete life is necessary for the great life. It is one in which you close the loop on all things. You know what we mean - complete all the incompletes in your life. Incompletes are energy drainers and distract your mind from the real task at hand of creating your great life. Incompletes include not moving someone from the team who needs to go. Incompletes include not forgiving or not making amends. Incompletes include walking away from a discussion that needs to take place. Don't allow the incompletes to dominate your life. Learn how to close the loop so you can be a world class coach of a gold medal team!

In this Chapter we identified the five competencies required to be a world-class coach. First, world-class coaches learn from their mistakes. Second, world-class coaches have solid interpersonal skills. Third, world-class coaches are open to new ideas. Fourth, world-class coaches are accountable. Finally, world-class coaches take initiative.

We also identified the five actions required to have a gold medal team. First, you must periodically assess your talent, but at least at the end of every "season". This process requires asking, "Does this team member move me forward?" As you answer this question, remember to look out for emotional vampires, drama queens and kings, firestarters, and crazymakers. Second, you must designate each team member's role: playing field, bench, or bleachers. Third, to assist you with this transition, remember to use the replacement strategies of *pick-off, AfterTalk, Force*, deflector shield, and QTIP. Fourth, courage is required to make the tough decisions necessary to run the team. Being coach of your team means being able to let go, forgive, set personal boundaries, be rejected, make amends, and have authentic conversations (complete the incompletes). Finally, you might require help coaching the team, so think about a new reference point or hiring a cheerleader. Combining the five actions with the five competencies to coach your team is the final key that moves you toward your great life.

CHAPTER 7

How to Use the 5 Keys

Many people have existed, yet never really lived.
—Elisabeth Kübler-Ross

In this permanent whitewater society in which we find ourselves, *winging it* is no longer a viable plan for trying to find the great life nor should it be. You have the power to create what truly matters most to you through application of The Great Life System. Understanding its five keys and their operation within the six dimensions provides a revolutionary way of looking at the major facets of your life, seeing what works and doesn't work, and applying simple principles to transform your operating system into a fulfilling one that you proudly call your great life. It is simple in structure and application, but founded on many years of research and theories. Its implications are limitless.

At this point, you have the *know* and the *how*. All that is left is to take action; to engage in conscious growth. There are two types of action. First is short-term action. Take short-term action by forming a team of supportive loving friends who will re-read this book with you. Support each other and be learning partners as you work through the tools, strategies, and resources offered here to continue to define what it is you truly want out of life. You will be interested to learn what your friends' value and how that motivates them.

The second action is long term. Take long-term action by practicing the skills learned from the 5 keys. World-class coaches make and keep a regular practice schedule and game plan. Elite athletes practice every day. Marriott, Nilsson, and Sirak (2007) discuss three types of practices that are applicable to the great life: warm-up practice, maintenance practice, and preparation practice. A warm-up practice "is exactly that—to warm up the muscles, engage the mind, and create confidence" (p. xxiii). A maintenance practice keeps you performing efficiently. This practice is a focused one where you work on something specific. The final type of practice is the preparation practice. "Preparation practice is also exactly what the name says. It is about preparing for the future" (p. xxv). While each practice has a different intention, they all have the same ultimate objective: to make life a great experience!

You can engage in these practices by using The Great Life Playbook that offers you a daily game plan (available on our website at www.5greatkeys.com). This Playbook calls for a warm-up practice each morning. As part of this morning practice, engage in the following activities:

1. Review your vision and your five values (keep those front and center).

2. Engage in quiet contemplation.

3. Restate a positive affirmation or your daily mantra.

4. Mentally rehearse how you want your day to unfold.

5. Organize the day and set goals for the day that move you toward your great life.

A maintenance practice is part of the daily game plan, too. This practice takes place each evening before going to bed. To keep performing efficiently, and reduce buildup on your karmic scrap heap, engage in the following activities:

1. Review your day to acknowledge successes (something you did that moved you forward, being nice to someone, or helping someone).

2. Review your day to acknowledge the "mistakes" you made and lessons that can be learned from that experience.

3. Practice forgiveness.

4. Review your day to acknowledge the fun you had.

5. Practice loving yourself through positive affirmations.

The space in between these daily and evening practices is *game time*. It is when you are taking action on what you have been learning during practice time.

A preparation practice, when you are planning for your future, occurs each Saturday. This is the day when you examine your behavior for the week and ask if you lived in alignment with your top five values this week. Use this practice time to reflect on whether any course correction is necessary. A preparation practice also occurs every six months. Semi-annually or annually, the Playbook requires an evaluation of your vision, goals, values, and teammates to confirm that these items are aligned and support the great life you are building.

Going about the work of your great life is not a straight line. Course correction will be necessary and The Great Life Playbook allows you to see that and make the necessary changes to keep you marching toward the great life. This Playbook also allows you to continue to choose your results, embody your results, receive your results, and acknowledge your results.

Posner (2008) wrote an essay on *Rapid Progress in Life by Consciously following a Process of Rapid Growth & Accomplishment* that explains the value and significance of *The 5 Keys to the Great Life*:

> Normally when we make progress in life it is because life presses on us to move forward. Rarely is it as a result of our own conscious choice and initiative. Over the long course of our lives, such forced progress occurs in unpredictable ways, sometimes through happy, but often through unhappy experiences; even catharsis. Surely, this is not the most efficient way to progress in life. And yet, that is the way the overwhelming majority of us progress in life. We call such inefficient, unpredictable, life-meandering progress "unconscious growth."

> On the other hand, conscious growth is the ability to use the power of our minds to self-conceptualize that which we wish to become, and then follow a process that enables us to turn that wish into *great* results and achievement. If we understand this process, and ardently follow its methods in our lives, we can achieve at ten times the level we are now achieving and we can do it with one-tenth the effort, and in one-tenth of the time. That is the overwhelming *efficiency* of following the growth and accomplishment, as opposed to our current *inefficiency* of growth and progress. (p. 9)

As you contemplate your upcoming journey to the great life, keep in mind Keith Harrell's (2004) advice from *Attitude is Everything for Success*:

> Life can be as simply put as this: Do nothing, and nothing gets done; do something, and many things get set into motion. We can't sit around expecting success to come to us—we have to break out of our inertia and take action to get what we want. (p. 8)

There is a secret to all of this and it is "to honor your nature and nurture your growth so you can maximize your ability" (Marriott, Nilsson, & Sirak, 2007, p. 2). The great life is worth it and you can do it. Take action today to get what you want and what you deserve. Your great life is waiting!

VALUES CARDS

Cut out these cards and use them to determine your top five values. We have left some cards blank in case there are values you would like to add.

Abundance Riches, good fortune, success and bounty	**Achievement** Producing powerful desired results; accomplishment
Authority Persuasive force; accepted control; recognized source or expert on a subject	**Beauty** Attractive or aesthetically pleasing
Challenge A call to test one's limits	**Change** To make different; refine; continuous improvement
Commitment To honor obligations; do what I say I am going to do	**Compassion** Selflessness; interest or care for another's welfare; desire to alleviate suffering
Competition Contest or rivalry to gain supremacy	**Cooperation** Working together for a common purpose or benefit
Courage Bravery; facing difficulty or adversity	**Creativity** Ingenuity; innovation; originality

THE GREAT LIFE VALUES CARDS	THE GREAT LIFE VALUES CARDS
THE GREAT LIFE VALUES CARDS	THE GREAT LIFE VALUES CARDS
THE GREAT LIFE VALUES CARDS	THE GREAT LIFE VALUES CARDS
THE GREAT LIFE VALUES CARDS	THE GREAT LIFE VALUES CARDS
THE GREAT LIFE VALUES CARDS	THE GREAT LIFE VALUES CARDS
THE GREAT LIFE VALUES CARDS	THE GREAT LIFE VALUES CARDS

Decisiveness Firm; resolute; taking action	**Discipline** Regimented; habit; behavior aligned with personal commitments
Discovery A new view or awareness due to exploration; productive insight	**Equality** Uniform treatment; parity; impartiality
Excellence Seeking the highest quality; commitment to the highest standard	**Fairness** Free from bias; rational; upholding equal values
Family A group of related people	**Financial Well-Being** Economically successful
Freedom Autonomy; to do as one wishes to do	**Fun** Merry celebration; amusement; adventure; playfulness; humor
Generosity Gracious giving without expecting a personal return	**Good Health** Positive wellbeing to include physical and mental health

THE GREAT LIFE VALUES CARDS	THE GREAT LIFE VALUES CARDS
THE GREAT LIFE VALUES CARDS	THE GREAT LIFE VALUES CARDS
THE GREAT LIFE VALUES CARDS	THE GREAT LIFE VALUES CARDS
THE GREAT LIFE VALUES CARDS	THE GREAT LIFE VALUES CARDS
THE GREAT LIFE VALUES CARDS	THE GREAT LIFE VALUES CARDS
THE GREAT LIFE VALUES CARDS	THE GREAT LIFE VALUES CARDS

Happiness Delight; joy; satisfaction; contentment; pleasure	**Harmony** Balance; good rapport; agreement among all elements
Honesty Genuine; straight forward; truthful	**Independence** Ability to make your own choices; free from outside influence
Integrity Discipline of being ethical & moral; acting with character and honesty	**Knowledge** Understanding gained through experience or study; information; awareness; facts
Love Warm emotional attachment; affection; adoration; deep caring	**Loyalty** Faithful allegiance; devotion
Peace/Tranquility Serenity; calm; harmony; quiet	**Perfection** The highest degree of proficiency; error-free; flawless
Pleasure Enjoyment; satisfaction; gratification; amusement	**Power** Influence or control over people, places, or things

THE GREAT LIFE VALUES CARDS	THE GREAT LIFE VALUES CARDS
THE GREAT LIFE VALUES CARDS	THE GREAT LIFE VALUES CARDS
THE GREAT LIFE VALUES CARDS	THE GREAT LIFE VALUES CARDS
THE GREAT LIFE VALUES CARDS	THE GREAT LIFE VALUES CARDS
THE GREAT LIFE VALUES CARDS	THE GREAT LIFE VALUES CARDS
THE GREAT LIFE VALUES CARDS	THE GREAT LIFE VALUES CARDS

Punctuality Conscientious of being on time; ready; reliable; prompt	**Quality** A standard of superiority or excellence
Relationships Companionship from fond social bonds; social connectedness; association with others	**Religion/Spirituality** Set of beliefs or practices organized around your faith
Resourcefulness Creative; clever; inventive; ingenuity	**Safety** Focus on refuge, sanctuary or shelter; freedom from risk or danger
Simplicity Clear; plain; straightforward; freedom from complexity	**Sobriety** Living without using any mood-altering things, people or places (nothing that takes me outside of myself)
Stability Steadfast; reliable	**Status** Prestige; position or rank showing achievement
Success Achieving goals; earning recognition, honors, wealth, position or rewards	**Tolerance** Open-minded; enduring

THE GREAT LIFE VALUES CARDS	THE GREAT LIFE VALUES CARDS
THE GREAT LIFE VALUES CARDS	THE GREAT LIFE VALUES CARDS
THE GREAT LIFE VALUES CARDS	THE GREAT LIFE VALUES CARDS
THE GREAT LIFE VALUES CARDS	THE GREAT LIFE VALUES CARDS
THE GREAT LIFE VALUES CARDS	THE GREAT LIFE VALUES CARDS
THE GREAT LIFE VALUES CARDS	THE GREAT LIFE VALUES CARDS

Tradition	Trust
Long established behavior; on-going pattern of culture; beliefs, or practices	Confidence; reliance; safekeeping
Truth	**Wisdom**
Authentic; candid; honest	Application of knowledge in a common sense manner; insight; good judgment

THE GREAT LIFE **VALUES CARDS**	**THE GREAT LIFE** **VALUES CARDS**
THE GREAT LIFE **VALUES CARDS**	**THE GREAT LIFE** **VALUES CARDS**
THE GREAT LIFE **VALUES CARDS**	**THE GREAT LIFE** **VALUES CARDS**
THE GREAT LIFE **VALUES CARDS**	**THE GREAT LIFE** **VALUES CARDS**
THE GREAT LIFE **VALUES CARDS**	**THE GREAT LIFE** **VALUES CARDS**
THE GREAT LIFE **VALUES CARDS**	**THE GREAT LIFE** **VALUES CARDS**

APPENDIX

Bibliography

1. Arango, J. B. (1998). *Helping Non Profits Become More Effective*. Algodones Associates Inc. http://www.algodonesassociates.com/planning/Mental%20models.pdf.

2. Anderson, B. *Leadership: Uncommon Sense*. Retrieved on March 31, 2009, from: http://www.theleadershipcircle.com/site/pdf/pp-leadership-uncommon-sense.pdf.

3. Anderson, B. (2006). *Playing the Quantum Field*. Novato, CA: New World Library.

4. Braden, G. (2007). *The Divine Matrix: Bridging Time, Space, Miracles, and Belief*. Carlsbad, CA: Hay House.

5. Cameron, J. (2002). *The Artist's Way*. New York, NY: Jeremy P. Tarcher/Putnam.

6. Canfield, J. (2007). *Maximum Confidence: Ten Secrets of Extreme Self-Esteem*. New York, NY: Simon & Schuster Adult Publishing Group.

7. Carnegie, D. (1982). *How To Win Friends and Influence People*. New York, NY: Pocket Books.

8. Castle, V. (2007). *The Trance of Scarcity: Stop Holding Your Breath and Start Living Your Life*. San Francisco, CA: Berrett-Koehler Publishers, Inc.

9. Chödron, P. (2005). *Getting UNStuck*. Boulder, CO: Sounds True.

10. Chopra, D. (1994). *The Seven Spiritual Laws of Success*. San Rafael, CA: Amber-Allen Publishing.

11. Comaford-Lynch, C. (2007). *Rules for Renegades*. New York, NY: McGraw-Hill.

12. Comfort, L.K., Sungo, Y., Johnson, D., & Dunn, M. (2001). Complex Systems in crisis: anticipation and resilience in dynamic environments. *Journal of Contingencies and Crisis Management, 9*(3), 144-158.

13. Cordeiro, W. (2001) *Attitudes that Attract Success: You are only one attitude away from a great life.* Ventura, CA: Regal Books.

14. Cordova, K. (2003). *Let Go, Let Miracles Happen: The art of spiritual surrender.* Boston, MA: Conari Press.

15. Craik, K.J.W. (1943). *The Nature of Explanation.* Cambridge UK: Cambridge University Press.

16. Das, Lama Surya. (2000). *Awakening to the Sacred: Creating a Personal Spiritual Life.* New York, NY: Broadway Books.

17. Das, Lama Surya. (2004). *Letting Go of the Person You Used to Be: Lessons on Change, Loss, And Spiritual Transformation.* New York, NY: Broadway Books.

18. Dictionary.com. Retrieved on March 31, 2009, from http://dictionary. reference.com/browse/key.

19. Drucker, P. F. (1998). *Managing in a Time of Great Change.* New York, NY: Truman Talley Books/Plume.

20. Dyer, W. (2007). *Change Your Thoughts—Change Your Life: Living the Wisdom of the Tao.* Carlsbad, CA: Hay House.

21. Ecker, T. H. (2005). *Secrets of the Millionaire Mind.* New York, NY: Harper Collins Publisher.

22. Franklin, B. (1964). *The Autobiography of Benjamin Franklin.* New Haven, CT: Yale University Press.

23. Fritz, R. (1989) *The Path of Least Resistance: Learning to Become the Creative Force in Your Own Life.* New York, NY: Fawcett Books.

24. Fritz, R. (1991). *Creating.* New York, NY: Fawcett Columbine.

25. Gawain, S. (2000). *Creating True Prosperity.* Novato, CA: Nataraj Publishing.

26. Gentner, D., & Stevens, A.L. (Ed.). (1983). *Mental Models.* Hillsdale, NJ: Lawrence Erlbaum Associates.

27. Greene, B. (2005). *The Elegant Universe.* New York, NY: Vintage Books.

28. Harrell, K.D. (2004). *Attitude is Everything for Success.* Carlsbad, CA: Hay House.

29. Harris, H. (2007). *The Twelve Universal Laws of Success.* Wilmington, NC: LifeSkills® Institute, Inc.

30. Johnson-Laird, P.N. (1983). *Mental Models - Towards a Cognitive Science of Language, Inference and Consciousness.* Cambridge, MA: Harvard University Press.

31. Jordan, E. B. (2007). *The Laws of Thinking.* Carlsbad, CA: Hay House.

32. Just, S., & Flynn, C. (2005). *Complete Idiot's Guide to Creative Visualization.* New York, NY: Alpha Books.

33. Kornfield, J. (2004). *The Art of Forgiveness, Lovingkindness, and Peace.* New York, NY: Bantam.

34. Kübler-Ross, E., & Kessler, D. (2003). *Life Lessons.* New York, NY: Scribner.

35. Maltz, M., & Kennedy, D. *The New-Psycho-Cybernetics: A Mind Technology for Living Your Life Without Limit.* Niles, IL: Nightingale-Conant.

36. Marriott, L; Nilsson, P; & Sirak, R. (2007). *The Game Before The Game: The Perfect 30-Minute Practice.* New York, NY: Gotham Books.

37. Maxwell, J. C. (2008). *Leadership Gold.* Nashville, TN: Thomas Nelson.

38. McDaniel, S. (November 2008). What's Your Idea of a Mental Model? *Boxes and Arrows*, xx-xx¶¶1-19.

39. Misner, I., & Morgan, D. (2004). *Masters of Success.* New York, New York: McGraw Hill.

40. Myss, C. (2007). *Your Power to Create.* Boulder, CO: Sounds True.

41. Newberry, T. (2007). *Success is Not an Accident.* Carol Stream, IL: Tyndale House Publishers.

42. Posner, R. (2008). *A New Way of Living: Essays on Human Evolution & Transformation.* Lulu, Inc.

43. Ruiz, Don Miguel. (1997). *The Four Agreements: Toltec Wisdom Book.* San Rafael, CA: Amber-Allen Publishing.

44. Senge, P.M. (1994). *The Fifth Discipline.* New York, NY: Currency

Doubleday.

45. Senge, P.M., Kleiner, A., Roberts, C., Ross, R., & Smith, B. (1994). *The Fifth Discipline Fieldbook*. New York, NY: Doubleday.

46. Scott, Susan. (2004). *Fierce Conversations*. New York, NY: The Berkley Publishing Group.

47. Sharma, R. (2006). *Who Will Cry When You Die?* Carlsbad, CA: Hay House.

48. Sharma, Robin. (2008). *The Greatness Guide*. New York, NY: Harper Collins Publishers.

49. Taylor, S. A. (2007). *Quantum Success: The Astounding Science of Wealth and Happiness*. Carlsbad, CA: Hay House.

50. Toffler, A. (1980). *The third wave*. New York, NY: William Morrow and Company, Inc.

51. Tolle, E. (2004). *The Power of Now: A Guide to Spiritual Enlightment*. Novato, CA: New World Library.

52. Tolle, E. (2006). *A New Earth: Awakening to Your Life's Purpose*. New York, NY: Penguin Group.

53. Vance, M., & Deacon, D. (1995). *Think Out of the Box*. Franklin Lakes, NJ: Career Press.

54. Virtue, D. (2006). *Divine Magic: The Seven Sacred Secrets of Manifestation*. Carlsbad, CA: Hay House.

55. Webster, R. (2006). *Creative Visualization for Beginners*. Woodbury, MN: Llewellyn Worldwide, LTD.

56. White, J. (2008). *I Will Not Be Broken*. New York, NY: St. Martin's Press.

57. Winget, L. (2009*). People are Idiots and I Can Prove It*. New York, NY: Gotham Books.

58. Woodruff, B. (2008). Interview with John Edwards. Retrieved on March 31, 2009, from http://abcnews.go.com/Blotter/story?id=5441195&page=1.

59. Zenger, J. H., & Folkman, J. (2002). *The Extraordinary Leader: Turning Good Managers into Great Leaders*. New York, NY: McGraw-Hill.

KEY NOTES

KEY NOTES

KEY NOTES

KEY NOTES

Printed in the United States
146686LV00002B/3/P